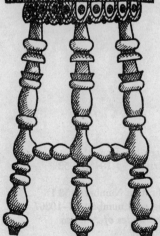

TOO OLD TO LEARN?

Robert A. Proctor

BROADMAN PRESS
NASHVILLE, TENNESSEE

© Copyright 1967 • BROADMAN PRESS
All rights reserved
422–306

Scripture references are from the
Revised Standard Version. © 1946, 1952

Dewey Decimal Classification Number: 153.1
Library of Congress catalog card number: 67–10307
Printed in the United States of America
14.N66K.SP

TO MY WIFE
DORIS EARLE
WHOSE HELP AND ENCOURAGEMENT
ARE REFLECTED ON EVERY PAGE

CONTENTS

TOO OLD TO LEARN?

1 LEARNING THROUGH THE AGES

It had gotten to be quite a ritual—Jim's scanning the morning paper and reading aloud bits of news here and there to Walt as they drove to work each morning. This morning was no exception. As he came to the section he called "hometown heroes," Jim exclaimed, "Hey, how about this! My neighbor got his picture in the paper!"

"What did he do, rob a bank?"

"No, no! He graduated from the local community college of the state university."

"What's so unusual about that? So did a hundred or so other guys. You mean he's in a group picture of the graduating class?"

Jim explained, "No, it is a picture of Dean Brown handing Mr. Thomas his diploma. The thing that is unusual about it is he's sixty-seven years old. It says here that he has taken some work in evening school ever since the college opened, then entered as a full time student when he retired two years ago."

"Sixty-seven! What does a guy that age want with a college degree?"

Jim continued to read: "Mr. Thomas, whose major interest was in social and political science, says two factors influenced him to complete his college degree. The first was enrichment of his own personal life. The second was his desire to be of more service to his community. He has been an active church member, a Community Action Commission board member,

and a long-time ward-level politician. He indicates now that
he may run for the state assembly next fall."

Obviously impressed, Walt replied, "Well, I guess that
proves you are never too old to learn and to profit from it."

As they drove on through the traffic toward the plant where
they both worked, they recalled other persons older than
themselves who had recently completed some learning project.

One of the section chiefs with whom they worked had
completed a flying course the previous month and had received his pilot's license. Also, the company had just sent the
head of the Engineering Department back to college for three
months, and he was *at least fifty*. Several in the last group of
persons to complete the leadership training course in their
church were *well over forty*. That seemed old to Walt and
Jim who were in their early thirties.

Adults are learning now even as they have been since before
the first one learned to write, leaving a record of his learning.

Before man learned to write, he had to learn many other
things in order to survive—how to procure food from the
plants and animals in the world about him, how to protect
himself from dangers and the ravages of weather conditions.
Long before Newton had formulated the laws of gravitation,
man had learned that he could not survive stepping off cliffs.
Unlike the birds he was earthbound.

In order to protect themselves against the capriciousness of
nature, families formed tribes. Then they faced a multitude of
problems in learning to live with each other. Adult learning
has continued partly because it has high survival value for
man. He makes progress as each generation learns from previous generations and communicates its cumulative learning
to the next one. Before systems of writing were developed
knowledge was shared and passed on orally.

Systems of writing probably developed out of a custom not
unlike the ranchers' practice today of branding their cattle.

One theory is that, as concepts of private property developed, individuals marked their goods with distinctive seals or signs. Out of this practice developed more complex markings, and finally as a by-product, man invented written forms of communication. Throughout history motivation for much adult learning can be summed up in the saying, "Necessity is the mother of invention."

Old Testament Learning

It would be difficult to say exactly when adult education began. Perhaps the Garden of Eden was the first classroom and Adam was the first adult learner. Like many adult learners today, he found himself with several teachers, God, Satan, and Eve. Many adults feel kinship with Adam in the wrong decisions they have made and in learning too late what they should have done. Some lessons are more difficult to learn than others and some are never really learned. Man still behaves as though he has not learned Adam's first lesson which had just one examination question, "Who is supreme, Adam or God?"

From the fragments of available evidence Israel's motivation for adult learning seems to have been different from that of other ancient civilizations. Among the peoples along the Tigris-Euphrates valley and the Nile River the chief reason for learning seems to have been economic. While this element was certainly present among the Israelites, their chief concern was learning obedience to God.

God's direct communication to Moses concerning the instruction of adults would indicate the importance of lifelong learning in the development of a nation of godly people. Moses summoned all Israel to instruct them in the "statutes and the ordinances" of God and admonished them to "learn them and be careful to do them" (Deut. 5:1). God commanded Moses to "assemble the people, men, women and little ones . . . that they may hear and learn to fear the Lord your God, and be careful to do all the words of this law" (Deut. 31:12).

A priority is suggested in the sequence of the groups of learners named here, "men, women and little ones." There were no formal schools in Old Testament times. However, the pattern for education is clear. The prophets and priests were the chief teachers, and they taught adults. These adults were then charged with the responsibility of teaching the children in the home. It was recognized that if the teaching of adults resulted in a closer walk with God, the children would more likely follow in their footsteps. Christian education would do well to recover this biblical pattern of teaching and training adults and equipping parents to be effective teachers of Christianity in the home.

The religious instruction of adults often played a major part in the revival of true worship in the Old Testament. One such incident is recorded in 2 Chronicles 34:14–33. While workmen were repairing the Temple, Hilkiah the priest discovered a copy of the book of the "law of the Lord given through Moses." As King Josiah read the law, he realized how far Israel had strayed and rent his clothes in fear and repentance. After Hilkiah consulted with the prophetess Huldah, the king then "gathered together all the elders of Judah and Jerusalem" to instruct them in the newly discovered "book of the covenant." As a result of this adult education movement, the chronicler records that during the reign of Josiah the people of Israel "did not turn away from following the Lord the God of their fathers."

When the exiles returned to Jerusalem following the Babylonian captivity, they found a city in ruins, physically and religiously. After the Temple and walls of the city were finally restored, Ezra turned his attention to instruction in the law of Moses. This, the religiously zealous exiles probably considered equally important. "On the second day the heads of fathers' houses of all people, with the priests and the Levites, came together to Ezra the scribe in order to study the words of the law" (Neh. 8:13). Then as this group of men studied the books of the law, they took action to bring about religious and social reforms. First, certain religious festivals were restored. This was followed by a public confession of sin after they had separated themselves from the foreigners in their midst. Finally, there came a renewal of Israel's covenant with Jehovah. "Because of all this we make a firm covenant and write it, and our princes, our Levites, and our priests set their seal to it" (Neh. 9:38).

In the wisdom literature of the Old Testament there are numerous references to both individual and group study. In the introduction to the Proverbs, the writer said concerning the instruction which was to follow, "The wise man also may hear and increase in learning" (Prov. 1:5). The psalmist recognized the need for long and diligent study of the word of God. He says of the godly man, "His delight is in the law of the Lord, and on his law he meditates day and night" (Psalm 1:2).

Two themes recurring throughout the Old Testament are voiced in Psalm 25:4: "Make me to know thy ways, O Lord; teach me thy paths." First, the ultimate purpose of study, teaching, and learning is to discover the will of God. Second, in this pursuit it is realized that one's teacher must be God himself. Though parents, priests, prophets, and poets may be the instructors, God is the source of true wisdom.

Sherrill [1] concludes that, while the informal instruction of children in the Hebrew home led to an "emotional stability in religion," it was the "constant stirring up of adult thought" by the priests and prophets "which compelled the growth of ideas in religion." The genius of this educational system was that it established stability without developing so rigid a system as to make growth impossible.

The basic purpose of ancient Hebrew learning among adults was that individuals and the nation might know the will of God. In the early development of the priesthood, the duties of the priests were to discover the will of God and to communicate it to the people. The priests' chief function was to teach rather than to offer sacrifices, and even during later periods they were sent throughout Judah to teach the "book of the law" (2 Chron. 17:7–9). The offering of the sacrifices was an indirect form of teaching, however, which dramatically set forth the nature of God in a way mere words could not do.

Usually we think of the prophets as preachers. However, in guiding the adults of Israel in their search for knowledge concerning the will of God, and by interpreting for them the meaning of current events, they may also be regarded as teachers. The greatest contributions came from individual prophets such as Isaiah and Jeremiah, but there were also "schools of the prophets." In 2 Kings 4:38–44; 6:1–7 Elisha seems to have gathered around him a group of young men in training. There were probably many teaching prophets in addition to the writing prophets.

The teachings of priests and prophets were often in conflict, in both method and message. One might think that such conflict would render the teaching of both leaders ineffective. Sherrill points out, however, that this was a period in which great religious growth was stimulated as men struggled with conflicts and sought to resolve them. He says, "From the angle of education one would say that the most daring imagination could hardly have devised so stimulating a way for causing adults to learn." [2]

The Early Church

The main thrust of Jesus' ministry was leading adult learners to discover the truth concerning himself and the nature of the kingdom he came to establish. His teaching ministry seems to have been directed entirely toward adults. When children are mentioned in the Gospel records, it is always for the purpose of teaching adults (Matt. 19:13–15; Luke 7:32; John 6:9).

Much of Jesus' ministry was spent guiding a small group of twelve men in their learning activities. He also taught large crowds of adults, as when the multitudes gathered to hear him. His concern for individual learning is illustrated in the third and fourth chapters of the Gospel of John.

In Mark 8:27 to 9:1 Jesus introduced two truths which the disciples found very difficult to accept and to which he returned again and again. These lessons concerned the nature of his messiahship and of true discipleship. The master Teacher patiently guided these men through experience after experience until finally the lessons were learned. So with us in our search for truth about the Christ. The goal of becoming a mature person in Christ is never fully reached. It remains a constant, beckoning challenge to the growing Christian.

Jesus' invitation to those who would follow him is, "Take my yoke upon you, and learn from me" (Matt. 11:29). This is a summons to participate in the mission and ministry of his church. Manson says, "What he offers to men is not an academic doctrine but something which he has tried and proved in his own experience." [3] This trial and proving method makes Christianity a lifelong and exciting adventure in learning.

The emphasis in the Gospels upon continued learning is underscored in the history of the early Christian church. The very word "disciple," meaning a "taught or trained one," implies that such a one must be a learner. In Acts 1:15 the term referred to the 120 followers who were present on the day of Pentecost. In Acts 6:1,2,7 it refers to all Christians and especially to the new converts: "the number of the disciples multiplied greatly in Jerusalem" (Acts 6:7).

It was necessary for the apostles to spend countless hours

teaching the new converts who responded to Peter's preaching on the day of Pentecost the true meaning of being a Christian. "Every day in the temple and at home they did not cease teaching and preaching Jesus as the Christ" (Acts 5:42). These men had come out of all sorts of religious backgrounds; some were Jews, but many were pagan. Although we like to think of our nation today as a Christian nation one is continually made aware of the fact that America's behavior and basic value system are less than Christian if not in direct opposition to the teachings of Christ. The disciple of today must be a life-long learner.

Further evidence of the emphasis upon learning in the New Testament Church is found in Paul's writings, the epistles of James, Peter, John, and Jude. These letters were basically concerned with instructions to the new Christian. Under the guidance of the Holy Spirit these writers were dealing with problems of false doctrines and were teaching believers how to live their Christian faith meaningfully in their time.

Early Cultures

Adult education among the Greeks.—Of the great cultures known to man, the Greeks were probably the first to put a premium on education. This included education of adults as well as children and youth. Although the Greeks used books (our word "bible" comes from the Greek word for book), adult learning among them was chiefly through the spoken word.

Grattan [4] suggests several ways, in addition to general conversation, in which Greek adults were educated orally:

1. Public recitations of Homer. Whether they could read or not, Greeks were familiar with the teachings of Homer. So popular were these public recitations that gifted orators made a profession of giving such recitations.

2. Drama. In annual drama contests and festivals the Greeks witnessed comedies and tragedies. Both forms of

Greek drama had their own educative value. The tragedy especially taught the moral nature of the universe.

3. General literature. This was "published" mostly through public orations and recitations. Greek literature was written to be read aloud privately and publicly, and copies of any one work were necessarily limited.

4. Politics. The success of each political regime in achieving a Greek democracy depended upon the effectiveness of its program of adult education as much as on any other factor. The end of Greek education was to equip the citizen to carry out his political duties.

The Greeks made a lasting contribution to adult education in the development of methodology. The dialogue method, attributed to Socrates and used by both Plato and Aristotle, has been popular with adult learners ever since.

The Romans and adult education.—By the time of the Roman period two significant changes had taken place which had some effect on adult education. First was the emphasis which Rome placed on teaching the populace to read. By the end of the second century only an insignificant minority of the people living in Rome and other Italian cities could not read and write. Second was the growth of a "publishing industry."

For example, speeches by Cicero were taken down in shorthand, copied, and widely circulated. Public and private libraries developed, and their full effect on adult learning is impossible to know. Undoubtedly these libraries made it possible for many persons to study the works of men whom they would never have had the opportunity to hear speak. Grattan quotes Carpopino as saying that Rome never took full advantage of the potential of adult education. Leisure time was spent in entertainment rather than for education. He speculates that had Roman officials urged adults to use their leisure time in educational pursuits, the decline of the Roman culture might at least have been delayed. If he is right, this is a warning

about our contemporary culture. America needs to learn from
Rome's mistake.

British Beginnings

It is difficult to mark the precise point in recent history and
say that this was the beginning of modern adult education.
One possibility is the founding of the Society for the Promul-
gation of Christian Knowledge in the year 1698. The purpose
of this organization was to combat vice and immorality owing
to the ignorance of the principles of Christian religion. Its
activities included the establishment of night schools for
adults, the formation of libraries, and the distribution of
books. While its major concern was children of the poor, the
Society also sought to teach adults to read and understand the
catechism of the Church of England and to read the Bible.

The founding of this Society was certainly one of the factors
leading to the seventeenth-century campaigns for adult literacy in Britain. These literacy campaigns were basic to adult
education programs which have developed since. Most adult
education efforts today assume an ability to read and write.

Even into the nineteenth century there were many in the
upper classes who were not convinced that the lower classes
should be educated. Some feared, for example, that teaching
poor adults to write would result in a great wave of forgery. It
was also significant that it usually was Christian concern that
prompted the desire to teach illiterate adults to read and
write. Often the teacher was a pastor who wanted men and
women to be able to read the Bible for assurance of their
salvation.

Such a man was Rev. Griffith Jones of Wales! [5] He not only
taught men and women to read, but he also trained others
who traveled throughout Wales teaching wherever they found
a group of interested, illiterate adults. His aim was to teach
them to read Bishop Morgan's version of the Welsh Bible; his

basic motive was the salvation of men's souls. A recent Welsh historian has said that it would be impossible to overestimate the value of Jones's work. Under his direction almost 3,500 schools were conducted over a thirty-year period. Perhaps as many as a quarter of a million people of all ages attended these schools. Yet, Jones did not start this work until he was forty-eight years of age!

John Wesley became interested in teaching adults to read and write in order that they might read the Bible for themselves. However, he soon faced a problem: having learned to read, what were the people to read besides the Bible and a few Methodist tracts? To solve this problem, Wesley developed an extensive publication enterprise. Methodist churches became the distribution channels for this popular literature, and every preacher "became a book agent." [6]

Grattan comments that "Wesley's activities illustrate a point that remains valid to the present day: the popular press is or can be an educator of the highest power. Everything turns on what is popularly offered and what selection from the miscellaneous offerings literate men and women are moved to make." [7]

All these educational efforts in England included both children and adults. About the summer of 1811 a school was established exclusively for adults. It also was the effort of a Welsh preacher, Rev. Thomas Charles of Bala. This movement soon spread throughout the British Isles. By 1815 there were at least seventeen such schools in England alone.

Even the briefest history of British adult education must mention the mechanics' institutes that sprang up during the nineteenth century. These schools were certainly above the level of literacy schools. Mathematics and various applied sciences were taught in order to give mechanics the scientific principles underlying their trades. Beyond this, many schools branched out into what might be called popular liberal arts.

While these schools did not give skill or training in the vocations, most of those that survived became technical schools. Some even evolved into colleges. For example, Birkbeck College of the University of London grew out of the London Mechanics' Institute.

In an analysis of adult education in England in the 1850's by James Hole, three principles were set forth which are still recognized as valid today: learning is a lifelong process; education must begin where a person is now; teaching by discussion is more effective than using the lecture method exclusively.[8]

American Developments

Colonial times.—A basic belief of American democracy is the educability of the masses. Our founding fathers felt that one requirement for a republican form of government was an educated and informed electorate. Since colonial times there has been public concern for the education of all people of all ages. Hence, the education of adults did not have the hindrances which it had to overcome in England.

One of the earliest organized efforts toward guiding adult learning was through the well-known New England town meeting. Here, lectures, speeches, and open forums guided the formation of political opinion and encouraged political action.

Adult literacy education was also a major concern of the colonists. As in England, the motivation was religious. The purpose of learning to read was to be able to read the Bible. During this period many pastors played double roles of preacher and teacher in their communities. Although the reason for learning to read and write changed after the Revolutionary War, the belief in the importance of a literate population did not.

After the United States became an independent nation, an

unending stream of immigrants came to her shores. The great need in adult education during more than a century following was citizenship education for these new Americans. Classes in the English language and in local, state, and federal government were most popular. These became mostly evening schools, and some were referred to as "moonlight schools."

Religion has been both a direct and indirect influence throughout the exciting story of lifelong learning in America. In 1710 the famous New England preacher Cotton Mather published a book entitled *Essays to Do Good.* In this book he suggested neighborhood benefit societies sponsored by local churches. These were to be discussion groups. To guide and stimulate discussion, he suggested a list of questions to be reviewed at each meeting. These had to do with the general betterment of the community.

This idea struck the fancy of Benjamin Franklin. When he organized his Leather Apron Society, a discussion club of twelve men, in 1727, it was patterned after Mather's idea. Franklin's group met weekly to discuss "morals, politics, or natural philosophy." Later the name was changed to Junto, and both membership and topics were expanded. The Junto has maintained a continuous, albeit sometimes tenuous, existence until today. Since its revival and rejuvenation by the city of Philadelphia in 1941, it has become one of the largest independent adult learning institutions. Its motto is "Fun in Learning." Gratton gives to Franklin the honor of being America's "patron saint of adult education." [9] He is certainly a shining example of the potential of adult self-education through private study and group discussion.

Nineteenth-century developments.—As the young nation struggled to establish itself during the first third of the nineteenth century, there were but few innovations in adult teaching.

At least two of these were distinctly Christian. The American Bible Society was established in 1816 and the American Tract Society in 1824. These groups were concerned with teaching adults to read and in furnishing literate adults with Bibles, tracts, and other worthwhile reading materials. Until the launching of the adult Sunday School movement in the latter part of the eighteen hundreds, these two organizations must be given credit for much of the Christian adult education in America.

This same period saw the establishment of many mechanics' and merchants' institutes and libraries patterned after, but generally more successful than, the British mechanics' institutes. One of the best known of these was the Franklin Institute, founded in Philadelphia in 1824, with its seven-point program for "the advancement of science and the mechanic arts." The interest of adult learners in popular science during this period was not altogether secular. It was generally believed that science would support, not contradict, religious beliefs.

If Franklin deserves the "sainthood" bestowed by Grattan, a list of nineteenth-century "saints" of adult learning should include Josiah Holbrook and Timothy Claxon, both of the lyceum movement, and John Heyl Vincent and Lewis Miller of the Chautauqua movement.

After being graduated from Yale, Holbrook became a schoolmaster. He returned to Yale to attend the popular science lectures being given by Professor Benjamin Silliman. After this, he himself became a popular lecturer on geology. In 1826 he projected a plan for a national network of local study groups. That same year he organized the first lyceum in Millbury, Massachusetts. Within two years the number of local lyceums had grown to one hundred, and by 1831 the National American Lyceum was organized with representatives from over one thousand town lyceums.[10] It was Holbrook's idea that the lyceums should address themselves to three concerns: (1)

mutual improvement of members through study and discussion; (2) establishment of libraries and museums; and (3) support the establishment of tax-supported elementary and secondary schools.

Although the lyceum movement started as local study groups, many of them eventually came to be simply the sponsoring agency for lecture series. For a period these were educational in nature and treated such topics as science, natural philosophy, politics, and travel. However, after the Civil War, these "lectures" tended more toward entertainment than to education. Knowles credits the movement with a lasting contribution to adult learning through the influence it had on the organization of women's clubs, civic clubs, parent-teacher associations, and the Great Books Program.[11]

When Timothy Claxton emigrated to the United States, he had already been active in the Mechanics' Institute of England. Shortly after he arrived in Boston in 1826, a Boston Mechanics' Institution was organized. Three years later, when a Holbrook lyceum was founded in the city, he was elected curator. He later set himself up in business manufacturing scientific demonstration equipment for the lyceums. Writing of the members of the Boston Mechanics' Lyceum, he showed unusual educational insight: "They now feel confident that the plan of having the exercises conducted by the members only is not only in accordance with the true Lyceum system, but far more productive of solid improvement, than the mere attendance upon popular lectures."[12] He says further that members develop better study habits, organize their material better, and improve their speech delivery by "doing it themselves."

The Chautauqua movement.—During the period between the Civil War and World War I there arose what Knowles calls "one of the brightest new stars to light the adult educational skies"[13]—the Chautauqua movement. Several factors that influenced the development of the movement include the

lyceum movement, the "normal school," and the Methodist
camp meeting. Chautauqua was founded in 1874 by Reverend
John Vincent, secretary of the Methodist Sunday School
Union, and a Methodist layman, Lewis Miller. It took its name
from the lake on whose shores the first Chautauqua was held.
The original idea was to provide educational training for
Sunday School teachers by offering short-term courses during
the summer.

With something of the spirit of the camp meeting and
courses patterned after the normal school, Chautauqua was
popular from the very first. So popular was it that it attracted
many who were not Sunday School teachers. Soon the courses
were broadened to include many nonreligious topics to meet
the varied interests of persons attending. One result of this
expansion was the formation of the Chautauqua Literary and
Scientific Circle (CLSC) in 1878. Knowles credits it with
being the "first integrated core program of adult education
organized in this country on a national scale." [14]

The original Chautauqua included at one time or another a
Teachers' Retreat for public school teachers, a School of Biblical Languages, a School of Theology, a Missionary Institute,
and a Church School of Church Work. The latter was a kind
of forerunner of present-day schools of religious education. A
correspondence, or home study, program was started by William Rainey Harper so that those who attended the summer
assembly could continue to study all year. Chautauquas
quickly sprang up all over the United States. Some were
faithfully patterned after the original; others were little more
than traveling tent shows majoring in entertainment. Grattan
reports over 10,000 Chautauquas between 1874 and 1894,
three-fourths of which were held in towns of less than 3,500 in
population. [15]

The influence of the Chautauqua was undoubtedly widespread reaching into many facets of American life. Some be-

lieve that the liberal political, social, and economic views of the CLSC influenced the thinking of such presidents as both the Roosevelts and Wilson.

Although Southern Baptists were never directly related to the Chautauqua movement, it is easy to detect an indirect influence, especially in the work of B. W. Spilman.[16] He became well known for his lecture "Laugh and Grow Fat," patterned after a type of Chautauqua lecture which was both entertaining and educational. While a student at the seminary in Louisville, he engaged his cousin as his "booking agent" for the lecture, the two of them splitting Spilman's fees. Later when he became responsible for the development of a teacher-training course, the "Reading Course" and "Lecture Course" resembled those of the Chautauqua. One of his early dreams was for a Southern Baptist Chautauqua. This dream was realized in the founding of Ridgecrest in 1907. For a while he even operated a Summer School of Theology at Ridgecrest not unlike the one on the shores of Lake Chautauqua.

Twentieth-Century Developments

It is difficult to separate movements in adult education into centuries. A movement may begin and end within the same century, but its influence may live much longer. Such was the case with both the lyceum and Chautauqua. Then, again, a movement that is deeply rooted in the past may take form in a later century. This is true of agricultural and home economics adult vocational education.

Agriculture and home economics.—Some forms of vocational agriculture education probably date back to Revolutionary War days. However, there was not a great deal to teach until the Hatch Act was passed in 1887. This provided for the establishment of agricultural experimentation at land grant colleges. The body of scientific knowledge about farming began to grow rapidly, much more rapidly than it was communicated

to the farmers. In 1914 the Smith-Lever Act provided for adult
extension education among farmers. To use a farm analogy:
the extension agent, an adult educator-demonstrator, became
the "wagon" that hauled information from the experiment
station to the farms. The county agent and his staff were
employed jointly by the state land grant college and the U. S.
Department of Agriculture. Cooperation of the local farm
bureau made it a three-sponsor program. Its success has been
amazing. More adults have probably been involved in planned
learning experiences through this program than in any other
adult education endeavor. Much credit is due this program for
increase in farm production year after year as the farm population has steadily decreased.

Public evening schools.—Tax-supported evening schools for
adults were offered as early as 1834 in Louisville, Kentucky,
and in Boston. The movement grew slowly until the last
quarter of the nineteenth century when labor leaders began
urging that the schools be opened in the evenings for the
working man. Between 1900 and World War I, much emphasis was placed on the "Americanization" of immigrants.
This program was strengthened in 1917 when Congress made
English literacy a requirement for naturalization.

After World War I, the course of study in these evening
schools was broadened and enrolments climbed. Evening
schools for adults reached their peak between-the-wars enrolment in 1930. Later, persons trained in elementary and secondary education were unable to develop a program adequate
for the needs of adults, so enrolment declined.

Many of the New Deal programs required the education or
reeducation of adults. Under these programs over 2,000 teachers received at least six weeks' training in special methods of
adult education. Out of these and countless other programs of
adult education during World War II emerged the professional specialist in adult education. It would require an entire

book to describe the rapid growth of adult education in the United States since World War II. A conservative estimate is that over half the present adult population is engaged in some more-or-less formal, continuing program of adult learning.

Southern Baptists and Adult Education

It has been said that one of the largest adult education programs in the United States today is probably the adult Sunday School program of Southern Baptists with an enrolment of almost three million. This certainly has not always been the case.

In the history of the modern Sunday School movement, Bible study for adults was a "Johnny-come-lately." Cope dates the adult Sunday School movement from "about the middle of the last century." Although he is not named, Cope says, "A Quaker in Birmingham, England, sought to do for adult men what Robert Raikes did for children." This man gathered men together for Bible study in "special, separate Sunday-schools." [17]

The organized class movement probably started in 1890 when a group of eighteen men organized the Baraca Class in Syracuse, New York. Similar classes were organized in other churches, and "the Baraca movement" spread. Several years later Philathea classes for women were started and grew just as quickly. For years national Baraca-Philathea conventions were attended by thousands. These classes proved to be both a boon and a boomerang for many churches. They were a blessing in that they engaged many men and women in Bible study. Class enrolments ranged into the hundreds. However, many classes came to major on entertainment and social activities rather than on Christian education. They tended to become "a church within a church" featuring spirited singing and expository preaching by a layman rather than real Bible study. The classes were strongly autonomous and often operated in competition rather than cooperation with the local church.

Southern Baptist leaders quickly recognized both the values and the dangers of the organized class movement. To give some guidance to these classes through study materials, the Sunday School Board began publishing in 1903 the *Bible Class Quarterly*. The classes remained independent of the local church, their first loyalty being to the International Baraca-Philathea Union. In 1912 the Sunday School Board formed the "Convention Adult Class Department" to "help secure and maintain loyalty" of these classes to their local churches. This effort seems to have been only partially successful. Acting upon a directive from the Convention in 1917, the Board started the Organized Class Department. Some of the objectives were:

1. The winning of every church member to active participation in the Sunday school.

2. The enlistment of every Christian in the full program of Jesus through the teaching of the Bible.

3. The proper relating of the church members in the classes to larger service in Sunday school and other activities in church and denomination.

4. The enrolling in the B.Y.P.U., the women's societies, the men's organizations those members of the Intermediate, Senior and Adult classes who are not, but of right ought to be, members of these organizations.

5. The winning to the Sunday school and to personal faith in Jesus Christ and to church membership the unsaved in every church community.[18]

Much credit for the eventual achievement of the third objective goes to the first two secretaries of the department: Harvey Lee Strickland, 1917–1924, and William T. Phillips, 1925–1952. After 1927, Phillips devoted himself almost entirely to adult Sunday School work. The millions of adults now enrolled in Bible classes which are integral parts of their local church's total ministry owe a great debt to these pioneers.

Like adult Sunday School work, the Baptist Adult Union of the Training Union had its origin in an interdenominational organization. Soon after the organization of the Christian Endeavor movement among youth was started, Baptist leaders recognized that a denominational affiliation was desirable. This concern led to the organization of the Baptist Young People's Union in America (BYPUA) at Chicago in 1890. Southern Baptists were members of the national organization and constituted a sizable majority by 1896. That year they withdrew and organized the B.Y.P.U., auxiliary to the Southern Baptist Convention. In 1918 the work of the B.Y.P.U. was assigned by the Convention to the Sunday School Board. In 1922 this department extended its age range to include juniors and intermediates.

During the 1920's groups of adults in many churches began meeting during the time of the B.Y.P.U. A variety of activities were included in their meetings. The most commonly organized studies seem to have been of the Senior B.Y.P.U. materials, or of the Sunday School teacher training manuals. In 1929 the Baptist Adult Union was organized and for many years enjoyed a phenomenal growth.

Training Union has provided opportunities for adults to study and to develop skills needed to be effective churchmen. Currently it is the educational responsibility of an adult Training Union to: I. Interpret Systematic Theology, Christian Ethics, Christian History and Church Policy and Organization. II. Give Orientation to New Church Members. III. Train Church Members to Perform the Functions of Their Church. IV. Discover, Recruit, and Give General Training to Potential Leaders of the Church.[19]

Unlike Sunday School and Training Union, missionary education for Southern Baptist started among adults then later was extended to youth and children. In 1885 the constitution of the Southern Baptist Convention was changed so as to prevent women from being accredited as messengers. This led to the organization of Woman's Missionary Union, auxiliary to the Convention. It has remained an autonomous, auxiliary organization. Throughout its history a major concern of Woman's Missionary Society has been to guide adult women in the study of mission needs and programs.[20]

At its meeting in Richmond, 1907, the Southern Baptist Convention, acting upon the recommendation of a group of Baptist laymen, elected an executive committee for a layman's missionary organization. The committee then formed the Laymen's Missionary Movement. Its major emphasis included education and promotion of mission causes among men, also tithing, and more liberal support of mission enterprises. In 1926 the name was changed to Baptist Brotherhood of the South and its education program was broadened to include all phases of denominational and local church work. In 1950 the name was changed again to the Brotherhood Commission of the Southern Baptist Convention, indicating a change in status but not in basic program. By more recent action of the convention, the major emphasis of the Brotherhood Commission is again on missionary education among men and, through its Royal Ambassador program, boys. Howse and Thomason say, "The heart of the Brotherhood work has always been missions and missionary education.[21]

There is not space to discuss all the learning opportunities available to Southern Baptist adults, but the area of extension education should certainly be included.

Shortly after World War II, Howard College (now Samford University) of Birmingham, Alabama, began offering courses in off-campus classes, or "extension centers," to better equip the noncollege trained pastor, and to aid laymen in their own Christian development and service. Baptist colleges in several other states offered similar work during the next few years. Later, the six Southern Baptist seminaries cooperated in organizing the Seminary Extension Department. This department operates extension centers in areas where there is no Baptist college extension work. Throughout the United States and in several countries overseas its courses are available by correspondence. Courses are restricted to Bible, church history, theology, and to the practical fields of religious education, preaching, and church music.

Recently the radio commentator Earl Nightingale quoted someone as having said, "If you are doing anything the same way you did a year ago, you are making a mistake!" He was emphasizing the changes so rapidly taking place in our world today. One dares not quit learning or he will be left in obsolescence. Man is on an intellectual treadmill. Learning must be a lifelong effort if one keeps up and continues to grow.

The Challenge of Our Times

In no area of life is there a greater challenge or need for lifelong learning than in one's spiritual development. The effectiveness and mission of the church of Jesus Christ is being challenged on every hand. Educational methods of twenty-five to fifty years ago do not reach, teach, win, or develop the men and women of today's world. Under the tutelage of the Holy Spirit, new ways of communicating the Christian faith to a world lost in sin must be developed.

This book is written with the hope that it will inspire its readers to make learning a lifelong adventure, and will provide them guidance in developing learning skills.

Only if one continues to learn can he know, in the words of Robert Browning, life's fullest meaning:

> Grow old along with me!
> The best is yet to be,
> The last of life, for which the first was made.

NOTES

1. Lewis J. Sherrill, *The Rise of Christian Education* (New York: The Macmillan Co., 1944), pp. 6–7.

2. *Ibid.*, pp. 9–16.

3. T. W. Manson, *The Teaching of Jesus* (New York: Cambridge University Press, 1963), p. 198.

4. C. Hartley Grattan, *In Quest of Knowledge* (New York: Association Press, 1955), pp. 31–32.

5. *Ibid.*, pp. 67–68.

6. W. J. Warner, *The Wesleyan Movement in the Industrial Revolution* (London: Oxford Press, 1930), pp. 230–31.

7. Grattan, *op. cit.*, p. 71.

8. Quoted in Grattan, *op. cit.*, p. 89.

9. *Ibid.*, p. 140.

10. Malcolm S. Knowles, *The Adult Education Movement in the United States* (New York: Holt, Rinehart and Winston, 1962), pp. 16–17.

11. *Ibid.*, p. 18.

12. Grattan, *op. cit.*, p. 153.

13. Malcolm S. Knowles, "Background: Historical Development" in *Handbook of Adult Education in United States* (Chicago: Adult Education Association, 1960), p. 15.

14. *Ibid.*

15. Grattan, *op. cit.*, p. 175.

16. C. Sylvester Green, *B. W. Spillman, The Sunday School Man* (Nashville: Broadman Press, 1953), pp. 26, 86–97.

17. Henry F. Cope, *The Evolution of the Sunday School* (New York: The Pilgrim Press, 1911), p. 174.

18. *Annual of Southern Baptist Convention, 1919* (Nashville: Marshall & Bruce, 1919), p. 470.

19. W. L. Howse and W. L. Thomason, *A Church Organized and Functioning* (Nashville: Convention Press, 1963), pp. 63–75.

20. Edith Clysdale Magruder, *A Historical Study of the Educational Agencies of the Southern Baptist Convention* (New York: Columbia University Press, 1951), pp. 30–31.

21. Howse and Thomason, *op. cit.*, p. 91.

2 ADULTS CAN LEARN

The state high school basketball tournament had moved into the semifinals. Walt knew Jim's morning commentary on the news would be a regular sportscast. Sure enough, he was right. Jim turned directly to the sports page as he closed the door of the car. He quickly found that the sportswriter agreed with him on a controversial call by one of the officials the night before.

Walt tried to defend the official, saying, "I'm sure he called the play as he saw it and was only trying to do a good job. Those guys have a tough time seeing everything."

"Yeah, but in this case the two officials even differed at first —one called a foul, the other a jump ball. Boy . . ."

Jim was already getting excited about the issue, and Walt tried to change the subject, "Speaking of sports, you were pretty good the last time our team bowled. You're going to pass me up yet." Both men bowled on the same team in the local church league. Walt had bowled since he was a teenager, but Jim had just started about two years ago. They had needed another man on their church team, so Jim had taken some lessons at the YMCA and had joined the team. He was in his second season.

Pleased with Walt's praise, he responded, "Yeah, I got with my old Y instructor and practiced most of last Saturday afternoon. I believe it's going to pay off. Man, I'll never forget the first session he and I had together. I could hardly keep the ball out of the alley. I was about ready to throw in the towel and call it quits! But he kept encouraging me, showing me how to correct one fault, then another. Of course, it took lots of hard work and lots of practice, but it has been worth it. I've really enjoyed bowling with you fellows from the church."

"You know what I've decided as a result of that experience? I believe that most people can learn to do just about anything if they want to badly enough."

Nodding his head in agreement, Walt said, "Well, desire to know something is a big factor in learning, I'm sure. You remember last year I was going to learn German through the educational TV channel? It went all right until they changed the schedule. Now German conflicts with one of my favorite programs on a commercial channel. I still believe I could have learned German if I'd stayed with it."

Jim started jokingly to raise some question about Walt's mental ability. Then, realizing that Walt was just agreeing with him, he replied, "I'm sure you could have if you had really wanted to."

Jim had pointed out a most important factor in learning—motivation. During the literacy campaigns of the nineteenth century, adults were awakened to the need and the values of reading. With this new motivation, they learned by the thousands. Throughout the ages, as man has felt a need and has had an opportunity, he has proved he can learn—by learning!

There are certain ideas about adult learning ability that are popular fallacies.

"You can't teach an old dog new tricks" is a common reaction when adult learning is mentioned. The saying is not true. A skilled trainer, using the proper methods, can teach a mature dog to act a certain way on a given signal almost as quickly as he can teach a puppy. Motivation, method, and opportunity are more important than the age factor.

This old adage is even less true of adult men and women. One of the earliest studies of the learning abilities of adults

was conducted by the famous psychologist Edward L. Thorndike and his associates at Columbia University. He said, "In
general, teachers of adults 25 to 45 should expect them to
learn at nearly the same rate and in nearly the same manner as
they would have learned the same thing at fifteen to twenty." [1]
Thorndike felt that the peak, or plateau, of learning ability
was reached at about twenty-five, then an insignificant decline
occurred during the next twenty years. After further studies
involving still older subjects he said, "A man at 65 may expect
to learn at least half as much per hour as he could at 25 (his
peak) and more than he could at 8 or 10." [2]

The adult who thinks he cannot learn will not find much
support for his belief in the findings of scientific studies done
during the last half century. On the contrary, he will find
evidence that he can learn anything he ever could have
learned if he wants to badly enough.

The saying, "They are 'sot' in their ways" probably had
more validity in the past than it does now. In a very stable
culture where few technological or sociological changes are
taking place, satisfactory styles of life and vocational patterns
may be established during young adulthood which are fully
adequate for the remainder of life. In this situation, adults
tend to resist change or to learn anything new.

However, rapid changes are occurring in almost every area
—from agriculture to astronautics, from food processing to
family structure, and from data processing to dating behavior
—and such rigidity is much less likely to develop. Persons in
such a society must be learning and changing continually.
They cannot develop in their early years the mature behavior
patterns which will be adequate for the rest of life. Two
examples from the writer's own family will illustrate this.

His grandmother, born in 1860, lived almost a century on
the same Alabama farm. After her marriage, a railroad was
built which crossed the farm. Before her death it was aban-

doned, and the rails were taken up and sold for scrap metal. Electricity brought changes to farm living. The country weekly newspaper gave way first to the radio, then to television, as a means of keeping in touch with worldwide happenings. During her infancy, slaves picked the cotton which today is harvested by mechanical giants. Could anyone become "sot in her ways" in the midst of such change?

In the next generation the writer's father recently retired from a vocational career as a master machinist. The equipment and methods used in the shop from which he retired hardly resembled those used in the shop where he served his apprenticeship.

The longer a way of thinking or doing has served one well, the less likely he is to see any need to learn a new way of thinking or doing. Few people in twentieth-century America have been able to maintain a satisfactory style of life without frequent change. Few adults have had an opportunity to become very "sot."

Advantages and Disadvantages

In addition to reporting his own research, Thorndike also reviews the work of others in his book, *Adult Learning*. They compared youths and adults in particular types of learning. In one study Hollingworth studied the relationship of age to three types of learning. One had to do with an exercise commonly used to measure the ability to use words or to learn ideas. Here he found significant difference in the learning ability of college students and middle-aged adults. His next study involved arithmetic calculations. These findings indicated slightly more loss of ability with age. However, on the average the middle-agers required only 12 percent more time to learn the task equally as well as the youth. The third test measured improvement in speed and accuracy of hand movements. Here Hollingworth found the greatest difference. In this case the older group required approximately 50 percent more time to reach the same level of performance.

A more recent study showed that, in understanding what they read and in the ability to learn new concepts and ideas, adults do as well as college students, up to about age forty-five to fifty, with a gradual decline after fifty.

Another recent study compared twenty-year-olds with seventy-year-olds in skills of memorizing, then recalling, material. It took the seventy-year-olds twice as long to memorize seven pairs of material such as "E × Z = G." Twenty-four hours later the oldsters could recall only three-fourths as many of the equations as could the youths.

From these and other studies of the relative learning abilities of adults, it is apparent that adults can learn. This is a most important finding. These studies also indicate that, like younger persons, adults can learn some types of material more easily and remember them better than others.

Adults can best learn material containing useful and meaningful ideas and concepts. They learn more slowly when it is necessary to memorize material, or when tasks involve fast and accurate movement of hands, feet, eyes, and other parts of the body, especially if coordination of two or more bodily parts is involved. While the adult has some advantage over youth in certain learning areas, he is at a distinct disadvantage in others.

Psychology of Adult Learning

In a review of studies dealing with the formation of concepts in children, Vinacke [3] concluded that the older and more experienced a child is, the quicker he learns a concept. Age and experience give the adult an advantage over youth in learning concepts until other factors offset this advantage. Vinacke further believes that the adult's task is not so much the learning of new concepts as it is the relating of new insights to concepts he already knows. Ideas, principles, concepts learned during childhood or youth increase in meaning and usefulness to the adult as a result of new experiences and learning. As understanding deepens, he is more likely to apply the concept or principle in his daily life.

On the other hand, from the middle twenties on there is a very gradual decline in the ability of a person to memorize new material. That is, material which has no meaning in itself and which cannot be organized into patterns related to past experiences. Not much of this type of learning is necessary for the adult. The fact that the seventy-year-old could learn such material is more important than the fact that it took him twice as long as the twenty-year-old.

There seems to be a peak in motor learning ability, such as sports activities, operating complex machinery, driving an automobile, which is reached some time during the twenties. However, past experience with similar activities may offset any loss of learning capacity, at least until middle age. The ability to transfer old skills to new learning tasks helps to explain how a sixty-five-year-old man learned something as complicated as flying an airplane.

In a summary statement of several studies comparing adult and youthful learners, Thorndike [4] notes that: factors such as the amount of formal schooling and motivation often favor youth; that when such factors are equalized, the influence of age alone "approaches zero"; that the number of "reports of superiority, inferiority, and equality of the adult learner" is about equal.

Scientific Findings

The studies of Thorndike have also stimulated other studies of the learning capacities of adults.

Herbert Sorenson reported a study in 1930 in which he compared college students (ages 17–21) with school teachers

(ages up to 55) returning to college for additional work. He
concluded that up to the mid-fifties there was no decline in the
learning ability of persons engaged in study. One group which
had been out of school for some time showed an apparent loss
when they first returned to college. In a few months this
disadvantage was overcome. It was Sorenson's [5] belief that
what appeared to be a loss of learning ability because of age
was simply lack of practice or of using these abilities. He
found that adults could quickly be retrained to use their latent
abilities.

Another study which caused considerable controversy
among adult educators was reported by Jones and Conrad [6] in
1933. They gave the *Army Alpha* test to almost 1200 persons in
selected communities in New England. The *Army Alpha* is a
mental abilities test developed during World War I to measure the intelligence of Army draftees who could read and
write. It is a "speed" test and most examinees do not finish in
the allotted time. The subjects ranged in age from ten to sixty.
The widely circulated and publicized conclusions stated that
learning ability increased rapidly until about sixteen years of
age, increased more slowly until about twenty, then a slow but
steady decline sets in. According to their interpretation, the
fifty-year-old was equal to the sixteen-year-old, and the sixty-
year-old had regressed to the fourteen-year level. However,
even this study, which is one of the most unfavorable for adult
learning, noted that there was no decline in the information
and vocabulary subtests. These subtests are now recognized
as some of the most valid measures of verbal intelligence,—
the ability to learn and use ideas and concepts which may be
expressed in words.

Irving Lorge,[7] one of Thorndike's colleagues, questioned the
validity of the conclusions of Jones and Conrad. His chief
criticism was that they used a test which placed a premium on
speed. First, he differentiated between learning ability and

learning performance. "If a person thinks the assigned learning task is silly," or if he concentrates too much on accuracy, "then, regardless of his potential ability to learn, his functional performance measured by amount per unit of time must show a decrement." He hypothesized that performance tests underestimated the learning potential of persons over age thirty and set up experiments to test his theory. He found no significant difference in performance between a group of men twenty to twenty-five years old and another group over forty when he used a test with no time limit. Using data from several studies he worked out a formula for equating the time factor in the test Jones and Conrad had used. When all scores were adjusted for the speed factor, he found that the men over forty had actually done better than those in the nineteen to twenty-one age range. He concluded, "Whenever learning ability is measured in terms of power ability, i. e., without stringent time limits, the evidence is clear that the learning ability does not change significantly from age twenty to sixty years."

David Wechsler, the developer of the widely used Wechsler-Bellevue intelligence tests, disagreed with Lorge. On the basis of his studies in connection with the development of a test for adults, he concluded that there was an increase in learning ability up to age twenty-five, but "even more striking than this is that after twenty-five our intellectual abilities are definitely on the decline," and that they continue "to fall off progressively with age." [8] However, a revised manual for the test published in 1950 reflects different conclusions based on later studies. It indicates that there is an increase in intellectual capacity up to about age thirty-five and that the decline thereafter is not as much as had been suggested previously.

One shortcoming of many of the studies quoted is that groups of young people were compared with groups of older adults having significant background differences which were known to affect test scores. In one study the group under thirty had completed at least one year of college, whereas the group over fifty had on the average an eleventh-grade education. A study by William A. Owens, Jr. overcame this handicap. During 1949–50 he gave 127 men the same test of mental abilities that they had taken as freshmen at Iowa State College in 1919. His results showed that all 127 men made a higher score than they had thirty-one years earlier. Their greatest gain was on the subtests measuring verbal intelligence—the ability to learn and use new ideas.[9]

Another short-term study produced similar results. S. C. Garrison retested thirty-two men and forty-one women with the Yerkes-Bridges-Hardwick intelligence scale ten years after the first testing. He found that every one made a slightly higher score on the later testing with an average gain of 1.8 (from 72.4 to 74.2).[10]

In a more recent study, comparing the performance on the total Wechsler-Bellevue scale of twenty-eight-year-olds with fifty-three-year-olds, the results showed that 46 percent of the older group did as well as the average (50 percent) of the younger group. On six of the eleven subtests the older group actually outperformed the youngsters.[11]

Many other studies support the evidence and conclusions already presented. In general, an adult can learn anything he ever could have learned if he desires to do so and is willing to spend the necessary time. This assumes that there has been no brain damage or deterioration which, of course, would adversely affect learning. A seventy-five-year-old person may require as much as 40 percent more time for the performance of some tasks than would have been necessary a half-century before. The studies also recognize that there are different amounts of losses and gains for the adult in different kinds of learning. Other things being equal, the adult's ability to learn ideas and concepts increases, up to age fifty at least. Beyond that the rate of decline is very slight. This knowledge is most

important for the Christian because these are the abilities he
needs most for continued growth in personal discipleship.

Motivation for Learning

Motivation and desire play important roles in learning. At
every level of education—kindergarten to golden-age clubs—
eagerness to know is a most important factor.

Psychologists classify motives as either "intrinsic" or "extrinsic." Intrinsic means there is satisfaction and reward just in
doing something. A baby does not have to be paid to learn to
eat. By the time most children reach first or second grade, they
are eager to learn to read, and simply learning this skill brings
a thrill within itself. Extrinsic motivation takes place when one
does or learns something because it will get him something
else he wants. A boy may mow the lawn, not because he
especially enjoys the activity but in order to get to go swim-
ming. A high school student studies, not because he has a
burning desire to know but to earn a good grade. All through
every period of formal education, both intrinsic and extrinsic
motivations are present.

In adult learning intrinsic motivation must be more heavily
relied upon. This fact is in favor of the adult, for the most
effective motivation is intrinsic.

Professor Gaines S. Dobbins has been an inspiration to adult
learners in many ways. Upon retiring from the faculty of the
Southern Baptist Theological Seminary after completing a
distinguished career of thirty-five years, he has continued to
serve Baptists of the world for another decade. While teaching
a study course in a country church, he was discussing the
problem of motivating adults to learn more about the Bible. A
farmer observed, "You can lead a horse to water, but you can't
make him drink." He was implying that one might get people
to come to Sunday School, but they could not be made to
learn. Dr. Dobbins' response was, "No, brother, but you can

salt the horse!" Dr. Dobbins was saying that it is possible to create situations in which adults will want to learn, and educators have proved repeatedly that this is true.

One other possible division, or classification, of motives should be noted at this point. In his wisdom, the Creator endowed human personality with certain *primary* motives— innate, unlearned, drives—such as hunger, thirst, rest and sex. These drives—necessary for man's survival—cause persons to seek food, clothing, and shelter, to protect themselves from disease and enemies, and to establish families. These desires are common to men whether they live in a cave or a castle, in the dawn or the sunset of a civilization. Man eagerly learns anything that will make his tasks easier or that will satisfy his desires readily.

The other group of motives is known as *secondary*—social, or learned desires. Not absolutely essential to one's existence, they may well become essential to his happiness. Most of the "status symbols" of today's culture fall into this category. This category also includes some of man's basic social or emotional needs. These may vary from one country or culture to another. Often included in such a list are: a sense of security; a feeling of belonging, of being loved and wanted; recognition both as a person and for one's achievements; a feeling of mastery— that there are some things that he does unusually well; and a desire for adventure and new experiences. Once a man has learned these needs, they become almost as important to him as his basic survival needs. Indeed, they may help to meet his primary needs. At times they may even take priority over innate drives, as when a man risks or gives his life for some cause in which he believes.

Feeling need.—An adult learns best when he feels the need for a change in his life. If he is satisfied with himself as he is, he is not likely to learn. Learning is not a pastime. It is often very hard work, and a person enjoys it only when his desire to

know, or do, or change is so great that the arduous becomes
pleasant.

Extrinsic motivation can become intrinsic. One study discovered that many young adults started coming to church for
social reasons. However, those who remained and kept coming
more or less regularly for a year or more became aware of
spiritual needs in their lives. Once this happened, an activity
that started for extrinsic motives was continued for intrinsic
motives. In these cases the first felt need was simply for
fellowship, not for Christian growth. This need (fellowship)
was met, and another (spiritual growth) was aroused. Ap-
pealing to extrinsic motives in order to involve people in
Christian adult education can be justified if they are led on to
intrinsic motivation.

If one would teach adults, he must understand what they
regard as real life needs. It is not enough simply to study the
general characteristics of adults; one must know the personal
needs of each individual whom he would teach.

Having a choice.—The adult learner knows something of
his own needs. He learns best when he can choose among
several activities and participate in the one he feels is most
likely to meet some need. The adult must have some choice as
to what he is to study. One weakness of many adult learning
programs in the church is that the adult has no opportunity to
determine the content of the course. His only choice is to
study one particular course or not to participate at all. As a
result, many adults come to an organization such as a Sunday
School and do not find a course of study which speaks to their
life's needs, so they drop out. A variety of courses of study
should be available to an adult through his church, and he
should have the freedom to choose among them.

Becoming active participants.—Learning is an active process. Active participation may be reading a book, engaging in a
group discussion, or being a part of a team project. Several

studies have sought to determine the value of a lecture alone
compared to a lecture combined with some other activity. For
example, a group of women heard several hour-long lectures
on the nutritional value of certain seldom-used foods and how
they might be used. Another group of women heard thirty-
minute lectures, then spent thirty minutes in small groups
discussing with each other how they might use these foods in
meals for their families. Several weeks later all the women
were asked whether or not they had used any of these foods.
None of those who had only heard the lectures had used any
of the foods. Practically all who had been in the discussion
group had used at least one of the foods, and most of them
had used more than one.

In sharing ideas, thoughts, feelings, attitudes, fears, joys,
doubts, and certainties with each other, adults become members of a "learning team." Each adult participating in a serious
group discussion is both teacher and learner. The experiences
he shares with others become more meaningful to him. In
most adult group learning situations (Sunday School class,
Training Union, Parent Teacher Association) each adult has
had some experience, or has read, studied, or heard something
that would be helpful to others if shared. Adults learn best
when they share what they have learned with others.

Knowing of progress.—Students from elementary to grad-
uate school eagerly await the return of test papers and the
issuing of report cards to learn of their progress or failure
to make progress. In most cases, adults do not receive report
cards, but they do look for some indication of progress. Anyone is encouraged by signs of success or discouraged by signs
of failure.

Several years ago the writer talked with an eleven-year-old
boy who had been sent to a state school for delinquent boys
because he would not go to school. The boy told how he had
not started to school until he was seven years old. The year he

was eight, he was out sick most of the year, and the following
fall he was put back in the first grade. The year he was ten
years old, he missed practically the whole year because his
father was disabled and he had to help on the farm. When he
was eleven, he went to a consolidated school. There he was
given a reading test which showed he was able to read only on
the first grade level; so he was sent back again to the first
grade. When asked why he quit school then, he replied, "It
just looked like I wasn't getting anywhere; so I got 'disencouraged' and quit!" Adults, too, get "disencouraged" and quit if
they do not see some signs of progress. Hendrickson says:

> Adults should be able to relate the results of each class period to the
> goals of the course or activity. At the end of each experience, the adult
> should be able to say to himself something like the following: "I came to
> this class to learn to converse in French. Tonight I learned how to
> pronounce and use in sentences twelve new words. I'm making pro-
> gress!" [12]

Having clear learning goals.—Adults just don't stay with a
potential learning activity if they cannot see clearly where it is
leading. Findley Edge quotes Dr. Gaines S. Dobbins in a
reference to an old Hambone cartoon in which the Negro
philosopher says, "One reason some folks don't git no whar is
dat dey wo'nt gwin' no whar in de fust place." [13] Often an
adult needs to clarify his goals. Once he is sure where he wants
to go, he can more readily determine the best way to get there.
As long as goals remain vague and indefinite, one is unlikely to
learn much, because of confusion or lack of desire. As the
Christian finds answers to such questions as God's will for his
vocation, his family, his community, and his church, specific
areas where learning, growth, and change are needed will
become apparent. He can then form clear, specific learning
goals. Once this task is completed, many opportunities will
become available to help him toward his learning goals.

Summary

For centuries adults have learned the knowledge essential to the development and survival of man's culture and to his very existence.

Scientific research in the past fifty years has demonstrated that adults are capable of learning anything they could have learned at a younger age. After a person reaches about twenty-five, a longer period of time is needed to learn the same task.

In adulthood a factor much more important than age is the desire or motivation to learn. The adult is usually involved in a learning situation because he wants to be. Therefore, he is often more highly motivated than the younger person.

Studies have shown that there are certain conditions under which adults are most likely to learn. Some are the same for all age groups. Some differ in importance with various age groups. Adults seem to learn best when they feel a need, when they actively participate in the teaching-learning process, when they know how they are progressing, and when they clearly understand their goals.

NOTES

1. Edward L. Thorndike, *Adult Learning* (New York: The Macmillan Co., 1936), pp. 177–178.

2. Edward L. Thorndike, *Adult Interests* (New York: The Macmillan Co., 1935), p. 2.

3. W. Edgar Vinacke, *The Psychology of Thinking* (New York: McGraw-Hill Book Co., 1952), p. 100.

4. Thorndike, *Adult Learning*, p. 31.

5. Herbert Sorenson, "Adult Ages as a Factor in Learning," *Journal of Educational Psychology* (1930) XXI, 451–459.

6. H. E. Jones and H. S. Conrad, "The Growth and Decline of

Intelligence: A Study of a Homogeneous Group Between the Ages Ten and Sixty," *Genetic Psychology Monographs*, XIII, 3 (1933), 223–298.

7. Irving Lorge, "Influence of the Test Upon the Nature of Mental Decline," *Journal of Educational Psychology*, XXVII (1930), pp. 100–101.

8. David Wechsler, *The Range of Human Capacities* (Baltimore: Williams & Wilkins Co., 1935), p. 106.

9. William A. Owens, Jr. "Age and Mental Abilities: A Longitudinal Study," *Genetic Psychology Monographs*, 1953, pp. 3–54.

10. S. C. Garrison, "Retests on Adults at an Interval of Ten Years," *School and Society*, XXXII (1930), pp. 326–328.

11. Homer B. C. Reed, Jr., and Ralph M. Reitan, "Changes in Psychological Test Performance Associated with Norman Aging Process," *Journal of Gerontology*, XVIII (1963), pp. 177–179.

12. Andrew Hendrickson, "Adult Learning and the Adult Learner," *Adult Leadership*, February, 1966, p. 286.

13. Findley B. Edge, *Teaching for Results* (Nashville: Broadman Press, 1956), p. 91.

CHRISTIAN GROWTH,
AN IMPERATIVE

One Saturday morning in late summer Walt stopped by to borrow Jim's spreader to fertilize his lawn. He found Jim behind the garage working in the garden plot that took up the back of his lot. Several small baskets filled with vegetables Jim had just gathered sat next to the garage. He was spraying a row of late bunch beans when Walt came around the garage. Walt admired the garden and said that Jim sure seemed to have a "green thumb."

"Yeah, a green thumb and a sore back! I have had a good garden this year, but it has taken most of my Saturday mornings. It's a real thrill, though, to an old farm boy like me just to see things grow."

Walt replied, "You can really see God working in nature as the seed sprouts, the plant grows, and the harvest comes— can't you? By the way, did you see in the paper this morning about those seeds that were found in one of Pharaoh's tombs in Egypt?"

"No, on pretty Saturdays like today I get right on to work around the house here. You didn't think I could start a day without reading the paper to someone, did you?" laughed Jim.

Walt continued, "It seems that those seeds were found when a tomb that had been sealed for about 3,000 years was opened. Some of the agricultural experts there planted them under just the right conditions. They sprouted, came up, and now the plants are bearing. Imagine that—shriveled little

seeds that old still having life in them! Under the right conditions, I guess a seed just can't keep from growing."

"You know, I was just thinking about the pastor's sermon
last Sunday on Christian growth. I guess a Christian can
shrivel up too—like those seeds. Just as it takes a lot of hard
work to grow a garden, even with good seeds, it takes real
effort to grow a Christian life," Jim said.

Walt questioned, "But didn't he say that the life really
planted in Christ just had to grow? I understood that once one
becomes a Christian, he has an obligation to study and grow.
This week I've been kind of taking stock and I'm afraid I've
not been cultivating my spiritual growth as well as you have
your garden."

Walt had raised an interesting question: Does a Christian
have a choice as to whether or not he will grow? Can one be
born again and remain a spiritual infant? It is possible for a
child to be born, live a number of years, and never develop to
maturity. This is always recognized as abnormal in the physi-
cal world. It is equally abnormal for a Christian not to grow.

Paul was obviously displeased with the church members at
Corinth for their lack of growth. He could hardly have chosen
more stinging words than when he referred to them as "babes
in Christ." (1 Cor. 3:1). When Christians today fail to grow,
as did those in ancient Corinth, they waste their time in
warring among themselves instead of witnessing to the world.

Nature of the Christian Calling

According to Edge,[1] when one receives new life in Christ,
growth is implied. It is the sign of life. However, while growth
in the Christian life is absolutely essential, it is not automatic.

Inadequate conceptions of being a Christian limit the
growth of some church members. For one, they see the Christian life primarily as membership in an institution, the local
church. They are satisfied to belong to certain organizations,

to attend services, and to contribute money to support the institution.

A second misconception is that being a Christian is equated with being a good American, or a good citizen. In other words, the demands of the Christian life are simply those of a social culture which has been influenced by the teachings of Jesus. According to this view, being a Christian is little more than conformance to socially accepted standards of behavior.

A third misconception is that the Christian life is measured in terms of what one does not do: "I don't smoke, I don't drink, I don't dance." A Christian should certainly refrain from some practices, but these do not constitute his major calling.

These views of the Christian life do not demand continued study, learning, and growth. They are probably responsible for many church members' remaining "babes in Christ" instead of growing to maturity in Christ. Possibly, erroneous views have kept some church members from ever really becoming Christians.[2]

In an effort to explain the mission and ministry of Christians today, the church has been referred to as the "New Israel." A study of the election of the nation of Israel as God's people may help to clear up some misconceptions of Christians.

God's call to Abraham (Gen. 12:1–3) was to receive a blessing and to be a blessing. Israel was to be the special recipient of God's revelation of himself and of his will. Her national life was to portray to all the nations of the world the character of God. This is seen in a personal way in the prophet Hosea's life which reflected the seeking, redemptive love of God. Also, Israel was meant to be God's instrument of revelation for the redemption of all the people of the world.

Because of the nature of this covenant and the mission of Israel, her people were called together repeatedly for the specific purpose of learning obedience to God's will.

When Israel ceased to teach her national mission to suc-
ceeding generations, she failed to fulfil God's purpose. Under
Josiah, a renewed study and understanding of God's law
brought Israel back, at least temporarily, to fulfilment of her
covenant relationship and mission. To receive and to be a
blessing required that each generation learn and keep God's
commandments. Growth was an imperative!

The Christian church, like Israel, is a people who are re-
deemed by God to be instruments for sharing his redemption
with all people and are to reflect his character.

Today God's special revelation of redemptive grace is in the
person of Jesus Christ. People who have accepted salvation
are expected to participate in God's redemptive purpose for
the world. As members of the body of Christ, they must share
in the mission and ministry of the church. God "gave us the
ministry of reconciliation" (2 Cor. 5:18). People cannot receive salvation and reject the mission.

Christians are to reflect the character of God as revealed in
Jesus Christ. The goal of Christian growth is "the measure of
the stature of the fulness of Christ" (Eph. 4:13). A Christian
should possess "joy, peace, patience, kindness, goodness, faith-
fulness, gentleness, self-control" (Gal. 5:22–23). These quali-
ties cannot be attained without continual growth. Perhaps a
Christian's attitude toward this responsibility is best expressed
in the Scripture verse, "I press on toward the goal for the prize
of the upward call of God in Christ Jesus" (Phil. 3:14).

The Teachings of Jesus

Many of Jesus' teachings imply that the Christian's life is to
be one of continual study, learning, and growth. Two parables
and a passage concerning the teaching ministry of the Holy
Spirit are selected for this study.

Three of the Gospels record the parable of the sower (Matt.
13:3–9; Mark 4:3–9; Luke 8:5–8). Its major purpose seems to

be to fortify the disciples against despair when men will not accept the preaching of the gospel. Various responses are portrayed. Some men, like the hard soil along the path, have so hardened their minds and hearts that the gospel does not penetrate their lives at all. Others, like the rocky ground, quickly receive the message, make an enthusiastic response, then soon "burn out." Luccock says that many Christians are described by the paraody on "The Village Blacksmith."

> Toiling, rejoicing, sorrowing,
> So I my life conduct.
> Each morning sees some task begun,
> Each evening sees it chucked.[3]

The seed which fell among the thorns pictures the life that is without priorities. Mark says that "the cares of the world, and the delight in riches, and the desire for other things" (4:19) simply crowd Christ and his demands out of their lives.

Most interpreters feel that "the good soil" represents those who make the necessary response to the gospel. These are true Christians. In the parable Jesus indicated the results of seed sown in "good soil"—it grew, produced, and increased. Christian maturity is marked by growth and productivity.

Jesus used another agricultural illustration to demonstrate growth in the Christian's life. When the farmer grafted new branches into a vine, growth and fruit-bearing indicated a successful graft. Some grafts do not "take;" no new life flows from the vine into the new branch. These branches wither and die and are cut off and burned. The teaching clearly indicates that the Christian is expected to grow and produce "fruit." "By this my Father is glorified, that you bear much fruit, and so prove to be my disciples" (John 15:8).

Christ did not leave the growth of his followers to chance. He promised to send a teacher. "When the Spirit of truth comes, he will guide you into all the truth" (John 16:13). The learner is to be a seeker after the truth, guided and taught by the Holy Spirit. The learner must be active in the teaching-learning relationship. He cannot sit idly by and expect the Spirit to reveal all truth to him without there being some effort on his part.

Perhaps an analogy will aid in understanding the role of the Holy Spirit as a teacher to the Christian. In national Carlsbad Caverns in New Mexico, or Mammoth Cave in Kentucky, guides lead persons into the deep caves where they may discover natural beauties of the underground. One cannot remain passively on the surface above and know all the mysteries of the caverns below; he must follow the guide and obey his instructions. The Christian must actively follow the leadership and instruction of the Holy Spirit if he is to discover the marvelous truths which are hidden deep within the holy Scriptures. Superficial reading will not produce much Christian growth. One must dig deep and follow his guide "into all truth" if he is to grow in Christlikeness.

The Priesthood of the Believer

A cardinal doctrine of Baptists and most evangelical Christians is the priesthood of the believer. In his first letter Peter says "like living stones be yourselves built into a spiritual house, to be a royal priesthood" (2:5). He refers to Christians as "a chosen race, a royal priesthood" (2:9).

The doctrine has two facets. The first teaches that Christ is the Christian's high priest and no other mediator is needed in order to approach God. Through Jesus Christ every Christian has direct access to him. A major theme of the letter to the Hebrews is the superiority of Christ's priesthood to that of the Levites. Christ abolished the need for the Jewish priesthood. Evangelical Christians have interpreted these scriptures to mean that human priesthood with special intercessory powers has no basis in the New Testament. This is indeed an important doctrine.

Another equally important facet is the doctrine of the priesthood of every Christian. Christians are to "offer spiritual sacrifices acceptable to God" (1 Peter 2:5) and to "declare the wonderful deeds of him who called you out of darkness into his marvellous light" (1 Peter 2:9). Paul says that gifts have been given to pastors and teachers that they might equip "the saints, for the work of the ministry, for the building up of the body of Christ" (Eph. 4:12). The recovery of these concepts has been responsible for the recent renewal of the New Testament emphasis upon the ministry of the laity.

The layman who believes that the responsibility to carry out the ministry and mission of the church is only for ordained ministers may see little need to study and grow. This is probably the view of the majority of laymen today. Ernsberger reports the result of a survey among Methodist laymen. Sixty percent indicated that their concept of the laity was "nonordained Christians whose function is to help the clergy." Only a small percentage defined the laity as "the people of God called to a total ministry of witness and service in the world." [4] Yet, the New Testament description of the early church indicates the later definition to be much more nearly correct. Trueblood says that "most Protestants pay lip service to the Reformation doctrine of the priesthood of the believer, but they do not thereby mean to say that every Christian is a minister." [5] However, he observes, "it does not take much study of the New Testament to realize that the early Christians actually operated on this revolutionary basis."

Edge insists that the "primary ministry of the laity," must "be performed in the world," not within the church building. [6]

Questions are being asked today: Is the church effective in communicating its message to the world? Are laymen effectively performing the ministry of the church in the world?

Most of the evidence seems to indicate that the answer to both questions is a resounding "No!" It is natural that there should follow the question, Why not? A frequent answer to this last question is that the average layman is not equipped or trained to bear a witness and perform a ministry which would communicate the gospel to the world.

If this is true, at least two responsibilities become apparent: first, the church and the ordained ministry must provide opportunities for study in Bible and related areas in order to equip "the saints for the work of the ministry."

Second, the layman has a God-given responsibility to avail himself of study and training opportunities which will aid in spiritual growth. The easy option to remain a "babe in Christ" is not open to the serious Christian. When he accepted Christ's invitation to salvation, he also obligated himself to share in the church's ministry. Commitment to Christ is a commitment to life-long learning!

The Epistles

In the close of his second letter, Peter warns Christians that scoffers and false teachers will come raising doubts about the promises of Christ, especially about his coming again. He advises them to live each day as if it were to be the day of the Lord's return, and to "grow in the grace and knowledge of our Lord and Savior Jesus Christ." (2 Peter 3:18). In a day when many are saying that the church is a failure, when a militant atheistic communism is rampant in all parts of the world, and some radical theologians are writing about the "death of God," Christians would do well to heed the apostle's advice. Peter places priority on "knowledge of our Lord and Savior Jesus Christ."

Paul also assigned priority to Bible study. "All Scripture is inspired of God and profitable for teaching, for reproof, for correction, and for training in righteousness, that the man of

God may be complete, equipped for every good work." (2 Tim. 3:16–17). Although Paul wrote these words to his young preacher friend, the power of the Scriptures is equally effective in the life of a layman.

However, it should be remembered that the Bible is not a magic charm that will transform and empower one's life by casual reading. Serious Bible study is a hard, disciplined exercise. It is more than simply learning more about the content of the Bible. In order to be a growing, effective Christian, one must constantly seek the guidance of the Holy Spirit in the application of Christian truth to every life situation.

A person who has committed his life to Christ must continue to grow in knowledge of him, in understanding of the church and its mission in today's world, and in effective participation in this reconciling ministry.

Lifelong learning is the Christian's privilege and responsibility.

NOTES

1. Findley B. Edge, *A Quest for Vitality in Religion* (Nashville: Broadman Press, 1963), p. 91.

2. Edge, *op. cit.*, pp. 77–82.

3. Halford E. Luccock in *Interpreter's Bible* (New York: Abingdon-Cokesbury Press, 1951), VII, 697.

4. David J. Ernsberger, *Education for Renewal* (Philadelphia: Westminster Press, 1965), pp. 29–30.

5. Elton Trueblood, *The Company of the Committed* (New York: Harper & Bros., 1961), p. 30.

6. Edge, *op. cit.*, pp. 101–108.

4 THE OBSTACLE COURSE

The day for the annual track meet sponsored by the associational Royal Ambassador organization had arrived, and it was a rainy one. The event had to be transferred from the high school athletic field to the National Guard Armory, located in a large hangar that had been built by the Air Force during World War II. There was plenty of room. However, since all the teams had practiced on outdoor tracks, none of the boys felt quite at home running, jumping, and vaulting indoors.

Walt and Jim each had a son entered in at least one event with the team from his church. As they met, Jim said that he was just as happy that it had rained after all. Puzzled, Walt asked why.

"Well, two reasons really. First, I remember last year. It wasn't raining, but it was cloudy, cool, and real windy. It took me a week to get over the cold I caught. Then, if it were a pretty day, I'd feel guilty about not working on my lawn. Jane says it is the worst looking yard in the neighborhood. This way I can relax and enjoy the games."

Each event was run twice; first, for boys eleven and under, then for boys fourteen and under. The first group of races included the 100-yard and 220-yard dashes for both age groups and a 440-yard race for older boys only.

The relay races were followed by the low hurdles for both groups, then the high hurdles for the older boys only. The Junior boys thought this was unfair until they tried several

60

times to jump one of the high hurdles and failed to clear it. Calvary Church, which Jim and Walt attended, finally took first place in both the broad jump and high jump competition. With a total of 56 points their church had finished second, and both men were proud of the boys.

By the time the meet was over, it had quit raining. Both men sat in Walt's car while their boys tried to master the National Guard obstacle course beside the hangar. Looking over the records, Jim observed, "The boys didn't do quite as well inside as they do outside. I guess the strangeness slowed them down some."

Walt was looking over his unofficial records on the various races and noticed for the first time that the longer races were always run at a slower speed than the dashes. He exclaimed, "Boy, those hurdles really slowed the boys down—especially the younger ones."

Jim chimed in, "If you think those hurdles slowed them down, look at them trying to scale that wall by climbing a knotted rope. They'll never make it!"

With that they decided it was time to round up the boys and head back for church and home.

Adult learners are likely to have some experiences similar to those of the boys at the track meet. If they have not been engaged in any formal learning for sometime, unfamiliarity will likely slow them down until they become accustomed to the new situation.

As a general rule, the longer the course of study the slower will be the learning pace. Like a "dasher" one can throw all his energies into a short term course, but he will have to "pace" himself in the longer ones.

Occasionally adults, like the boys on the obstacle course, undertake something beyond their abilities at certain stages of learning. Usually the obstacles can be overcome by reviewing material or by learning more basic skills first. Returning to the

advanced or difficult tasks makes accomplishment more likely
then.

Kidd says that "few, if any, have ever approached their
potential achievement in learning" and that "the stoutest
shackles binding an adult learner have little or nothing to do
with age; they are self-imposed." [1] What are these self-imposed obstacles to adult learning? How may they be overcome?

Emotional Barriers

One misconception about learning at any age is that it is
purely a rational or intellectual process. This probably can be
traced to the Greek idea of dualism—dividing man into mind
and body. Modern psychology has firmly established the fact
that man functions as a unit; body, mind, soul, emotions, and
whatever other artificial divisions might be made of him.

The emotional factors, or concomitants of learning, may aid,
hinder, and even prevent learning. The desire to learn exercises a positive effect on feelings about learning.

Emotions about himself, his teacher, his fellow learners, or
some other factor in the learning situation can effect the
learner. Negative emotions *may* have positive value in learning. A person who becomes frustrated and angry with himself
for slow and inefficient performance of a certain task may then
be spurred to learn a better way.

Self-satisfaction.—If one's present status is unsatisfactory, he
usually wants to remedy the situation and is ready to learn.
On the other hand, if one is satisfied with his present situation,
he is not apt to be interested in learning anything new about
it. Too many adults are satisfied with their present levels of
learning achievement and are nowhere near their potential.

The story is told of the farmer who could not be interested
in attending a demonstration of improved farming methods.
His reason was that he already knew a lot more about im-

proved farming methods than he was using! He was unable or unwilling to apply what he knew, at least in theory. This problem is a major barrier to further Christian growth. Many adults know more Christian principles than they have yet applied.

Why do adults become self-satisfied and see no need to grow? There are several reasons. Across the years satisfactory ways of meeting routine needs have been developed. Some adults must be convinced that improved methods are worth the effort required to learn and change.

Another answer is found in the choice of evaluation standards. In any area one can find another person about whom he can say, "Well, I'm at least doing better at this than he is."

Some Sunday School teachers occasionally feel a need to learn more effective teaching methods. But before any effort toward improvement is made, they think of "all the people who refused even to try," and settle back in complacency. Recognizing the importance of Bible teaching and the stewardship of God-given talents, a teacher should ask, Am I the best teacher possible for me to be? If not, why not, and what can I do to improve? The same question probably would cause most adult Bible class members to recognize their need for spending more time in lesson preparation.

A look at any one of several surveys of Bible knowledge among church members is enough to cause dissatisfaction with the status quo. An attempt to answer questions from any book in the Church Study Course series on Baptist doctrine, history of the church, or Christian home life should convince most adults of their need for Christian growth and learning.

In the congregation of a rural church was an elderly woman who had an uncommon concern about the quality of her spiritual life. At first people thought that she had only recently become a Christian and previously had lived far from the Lord. This was not so. From her youth she had been an outstanding Christian. Why then this deep concern which less mature Christians did not seem to share? She measured her spiritual stature against that of her Christ rather than people. The Christian who walks close to his Lord will always feel a hopeful and holy discontent with his Christian growth. He usually welcomes opportunities for learning.

Fear of failure.—The old adage "nothing ventured, nothing gained" can also be stated, "nothing ventured, nothing lost." If one does not try to learn anything, he cannot be counted a failure. Fear of failure may keep him from trying. What can be done to overcome this obstacle to adult learning?

One can seek the cause of his fear and test it for valid basis in fact. A common cause of adult fear of failure is the "prevailing view that he and all other adults are not efficient learners." [2] The factual evidence presented previously should be enough to eliminate this fear. However, if one continues to believe that he cannot learn, his attitude can have as much influence as if it were true. But, when the fearful learner will be encouraged by the experience of other adults, and will actually undertake and learn some new task, he becomes convinced of his own ability. If he wants to learn and has proper guidance, he is usually pleasantly surprised by the results of his efforts.

Another cause of fear of failure is the memory of past failures. Some persons are better able to remember a few failures than they are to recall many successes. But if they were to list learning situations in which they have succeeded over the last several years, this could help to overcome the fear. For other persons the reasons for previous failure may no longer be true. They should list the causes for these failures and try to analyze them objectively. Such a list might include inadequate knowledge, poor motivation, lack of needed help, needed material unavailable, or material that should have been learned in a group. If these former difficulties have been removed, one can now approach the task and expect to succeed.

Failure itself may be a way of learning; therefore, lack of assured success should not keep one from trying. A mature person learns from his failures as well as from his successes. This was classically illustrated in the life of Thomas A. Edison. After the great inventor had tried over a thousand experiments in his efforts to perfect an incandescent light bulb, a friend remarked that it was a pity that so much time had been wasted in the experiments. Edison's response was that the time had not been wasted at all; he now knew over a thousand ways that would not work!

Fear of rejection.—Persons have a basic social need to be accepted by their peers. This is especially true in a small learning group. One condition for good adult learning is active participation on the part of the learner. Yet many adults hesitate to express their opinions in a group. Leaders of adult educational organizations in the church often have difficulty in getting members to participate in a discussion. Lack of participation may be a barrier to learning.

Bergevin and McKinley [3] suggest two possible reasons for this barrier. The adult learner fears to reveal his ignorance on a given topic, and he fears to express a view contrary to those of other group members. By simply sitting and listening, he protects himself from exposure to these threats.

If a Christian learning group creates an atmosphere of mutual trust and acceptance, so conducive to learning, one who is aware of his lack of knowledge will find help and sympathetic guidance among friends in his search for truth. It should be possible for a person to express divergent, even "heretical," views in such a group and not feel rejected. Unless such an attitude prevails, much needed learning fails to take place.

Sunday School teachers who have been successful in creating such an atmosphere in their classes have reported that

questions raised and "off-beat" views expressed gave them
their most valuable clue to the learning needs of class members.

When one young adult finally found himself in a group
which he felt could be trusted not to "throw him out," he
raised a doctrinal question which he had pondered for years.
After the leader and group members had helped him to discover a satisfactory answer, he confessed that he had been
afraid to raise the question before for fear of being "branded a
heretic."

All members of a learning group have a responsibility to
help remove this barrier if it exists in their organization.

Poorly Defined Goals

The Stoic philosopher Seneca, who lived during New Testament times said, "Nobody ever became wise by chance." One
hindrance to effective learning is that many adults leave learning to chance experiences. Sound learning is not achieved by
accident or unplanned experiences. Such learning is inefficient
and is quite likely to leave great vacancies in the storehouse of
knowledge and skills. Time for learning is too limited for
adults to go through life learning by "happenstance."

Vaguely defined learning goals are little better than no goals
at all. If the average adult is asked why he attended a particular meeting of a religious educational organization, he likely
replies that it was to learn more about the Bible or to become
a better Christian. When asked further why he wants to know
more about the Bible or what it means to be a better Christian, he is usually without an answer.

To see the importance of clearly defined goals in learning,
let us suppose that a man set out traveling one morning with
no particular destination in mind. Starting in one direction he
continued to a crossroad where he turned and followed the
way that looked more attractive at the moment. Throughout

the day he repeated this procedure and toward evening found himself approaching a town. As he entered, several things looked very familiar. Then he realized that he was back where he had started. He had enjoyed the day's outing, but after spending time, energy, and money, he had gone exactly nowhere!

Imagine a second traveler who had always wanted to "go west." With this vague goal in mind he set out and by the aid of map, compass, and road signs, maintained a generally westerly direction. He crossed extensive but uninteresting plains, had difficulties crossing rugged mountains, and finally came to a barren coastline. His trip back was equally difficult, long, and uninteresting. He achieved his purpose of going west, but he had missed the beauty and grandeur of such places as Pike's Peak, Yellowstone National Park, the Grand Canyon, Hoover Dam, the Golden Gate Bridge, and dozens of other natural and man-made wonders. His general conclusion was that his trip was not worthwhile.

A third man's objective was to attend a conference in San Francisco. His purpose was to learn the latest techniques in marketing a certain product. He read several recommended books in preparation for the conference sessions. Having never visited that section of the United States, he planned his trip with stopovers at places he wished to visit. After spending the same period of time as did the second traveler, the third man returned feeling that his trip was most worthwhile.

The chief difference in these three situations was the clarity of each traveler's goals. With his goals clearly in mind, the third man very wisely made specific plans for their attainment and had a more satisfactory experience.

The parallels to learning are obvious. A person with no goals is unlikely to learn much for his little effort. Vaguely defined purposes usually result in a feeling that "it just isn't worth the effort." This feeling is intensified by no sense of

progress, and a person usually loses interest in an activity and
drops it.

Clearly defined goals help one to divide larger learning
tasks into more manageable blocks of activities. Specific plans
can then be made for achieving these subgoals. Each achievement is a sign of progress toward the long-distance objective
and furnishes the encouragement necessary for continued
effort.

A Lack of Options

An important factor in adult education is the opportunity to
select a course of study. This assumes that an adult has some
awareness of his needs and that, on the basis of past experiences, he can choose among alternatives the course which will
best meet his need.

Until recently most programs of adult Christian education
offered few, if any, alternatives. Therefore, adult educators in
general have been rightly critical of religious education at this
point. Most denominations have offered only the Uniform
Sunday School lessons for adults in Sunday School. Where
there have been other organizations, they too have offered
only one curriculum. The adult group had no voice in the
selection of courses, materials, or alternatives. The programs
spoke to the needs of some, and they continued to participate.
Others attended simply out of a sense of loyalty to the organization or to the church. Many others dropped out or were never
enlisted.

Fortunately, the designers of curricula for most major denominations in the United States have recognized this defi-
ciency as an obstacle to adult learning and have taken steps to
correct it. The Seabury Series, published by the Protestant
Episcopal Church, offers adults elective courses in six major
areas. Adults in Presbyterian and Reformed churches using
the Covenant Life Curriculum have several choices available

to them. With the publication of the Life and Work Curriculum in the fall of 1966 by the Baptist Sunday School Board, several choices in study units are now available to Southern Baptists.

In all of these and other recently published curricula, there is still the danger of centralized planning on the local church level by a board of Christian education or a church council. According to adult education principles, the individual learning group should be familiar with all available materials and should make its own choice as to which course will best meet its common needs.

Bergevin and McKinley [4] see at least four advantages in such a practice. First, if adult members of a learning group have chosen a course of study, they will feel a greater responsibility for its success. It now becomes "our" program, not "theirs." When a group is given a tightly prescribed program by a pastor or superintendent, the group is likely to feel that it is "his" program and will let him be responsible for its success.

Second, adults need an opportunity over a long period of time to discover their needs and programs of study which best meet these needs. Facing a choice between alternatives, the learning group must look for its real needs. Experience in choosing and in follow-up evaluations increases the ability to make correct choices. Every adult learning group, accustomed to being "spoon-fed" prescribed courses of study, will not at first be expected to analyze its needs and choose correct courses. Some may even prefer to continue with the old procedures, for this is the easier method. However, if programs of adult religious education are to become more effective, adults themselves must assume more responsibility for planning and evaluating.

Third, adults learn how to work together responsibly as members of a learning team by planning their courses of study and accepting responsibility for their learning. Many obstacles to learning will be cleared away. Adults will lose their sense of self-satisfaction; they will not fear failure because learning now is a group project, not an individual undertaking; they will feel accepted by fellow seekers-after-truth, and together they can clarify their goals.

Finally, adults who have used such an approach to religious education have found that participation in such a program has made them aware of deeper spiritual needs. A constantly changing, prescribed curriculum, designed for "Mr. Average Christian," does not provide time for depth study or analysis of spiritual needs. Adults who design their own programs under the guidance of a competent educator will develop into responsible learning teams.

To accomplish such a program, many adults will have to develop some new skills. The proper use of the Life and Work materials—especially those furnished by the Training Union Department—can guide them in learning these needed skills.

"How Are We Doing?"

This is a seldom heard question in adult religious education classes. Because goals have not been clearly and specifically defined, most class members assume that the purpose of Sunday School (whatever it is) is being met. Failure to seek an objective answer to the question Are we making satisfactory progress toward our goal? is an obstacle to adult learning. This does not mean that examinations and report cards are necessary, but written end-of-unit tests might be appropriate. Many goals of individual home study or of group study in Christian education do not lend themselves to this type of evaluation. Sometimes it would be better for a class period to be used by members for sharing with one another ways in which they feel that the group has achieved its goals or has failed to reach them. The method of evaluation will depend upon the nature of the goal. Evaluation is an effort to answer the question How well did we accomplish what we started out to do?

The function of evaluation in learning is twofold. First, if the goal has been achieved, the group is rewarded by a feeling of accomplishment and is encouraged to undertake more learning tasks. Second, if the goal has been only partially completed, evaluation aids the group in understanding why it fell short and what needs to be done differently the next time.

After the goal of learning has been stated, the procedure which follows is one of approximation-evaluation-correction. The first step is to plan a course of action designed to reach the goal. This is called "approximation" because it usually brings the learner within the *approximate* vicinity of the goal. "Evaluation" indicates how close to the goal he is. On the basis of this information, he can make "corrections" in action plans that increase his chances of reaching the goal.

The process of learning is like the flight of an airplane. The pilot starts out on a course which he believes will lead to his destination. After a period of time he checks his flight by a landmark to determine if he is still on course. If he is off, he makes corrections that head him back toward his destination. All along his route he periodically evaluates and corrects and thus is confident of arriving at his destination.

Kidd [5] suggests that one effective method of evaluation for adult learning is "feedback." He defines it as "the process by which, in any communication or any learning process, the recipient or learner is able to state what is his perception of the situation at any given time." Examples include: (1) stating at the end of the period what members of a class understood from a lecture; (2) stating feelings about what took place as well as facts learned; (3) stating ways in which the session succeeded or failed in achieving objectives and personal goals; and, (4) listing omitted emphases or issues that should be included in the following sessions.

The by-products of such a practice are: (1) "regular assessment of what is occurring leads to improved performance" and (2) "being able to measure his own success is perhaps the strongest motivating force for an adult to continue or to put fresh energy into the chosen study." Feedback may be obtained by having participants fill out reaction forms at the end of a meeting or complete detailed questionnaires later. Other devices would be a feedback discussion at the end of the period or end-of-course interviews.

Persons and Programs

The issue as to whether education should teach persons or content material has sometimes been too sharply and artificially defined. The purpose of Christian adult education is to teach men and women content material. Out of such study should grow knowledge, understanding, attitudes, and certain skills that can be applied in life situations. Taylor [6] points out that a needs-centered curriculum for religious education recognizes the necessity for knowledge of biblical content and the facts of Christian heritage. "Any curriculum that stops short of these historic truths—that is, focuses exclusively on contemporary needs—will always be less than Christian education."

Recognizing the importance of the resource content material provided in the curriculum, however, one must be well aware that the "major purpose of adult Christian education is to assist persons to resolve the problems which they face, the needs which daily experience identifies." [7]

Summary

As one begins the adventure of Christian learning, he likely finds some obstacles in his way. This is true of any worthwhile endeavor. Nature and circumstances have put some hurdles there, but most of them are self-imposed.

If the adult learner has "skinned shins" from continually knocking over hurdles, he may ask himself why he is in the race in the first place. Clearly defined aims and fellowship with a learning group will help to overcome many emotional barriers. The learner then is ready to use curricula and other resource material in pursuit of his goals.

By following the "approximation, evaluation, correction" technique he will confidently advance toward his goal.

NOTES

1. J. R. Kidd, *How Adults Learn* (New York: Association Press, 1959), p. 9.

2. *Ibid.*, p. 95.

3. Paul Bergevin and John McKinley, *Design for Adult Education in the Church* (Greenwich, Conn.: Seabury Press, 1958), pp. xviii–xix.

4. *Ibid.*, p. xx–xxi.

5. Kidd, *op. cit.*, p. 294–295.

6. Marvin J. Taylor, "Toward Better Adult Curricular," *The Future Course of Christian Adult Education,* Lawrence C. Little (ed.), (Pittsburgh: University of Pittsburgh Press, 1959), p. 223.

7. *Ibid.*, p. 224.

5 LEARNING TO LEARN

When it was Walt's turn to drive to work, he seldom had to wait for Jim. Ordinarily he was sitting on his porch reading the morning paper when the weather was pleasant, as on this particular day. Walt waited at least five minutes before Jim came running out with his tie instead of the usual newspaper in his hand. As he breathlessly got into the car, Walt asked, "Say, where is your paper? I'm not sure I can drive without your reading and commenting on the news!"

"Aw, cut it out. I'm in no mood to be kidded this morning. I just got up about fifteen minutes ago."

"What was the matter? Didn't your alarm go off? Don't tell me your kids overslept, too! I wish ours would sometimes—especially on Saturday."

"Oh, the clock went off all right, and everybody else got up on time. But when Jane called to say breakfast was ready, I was still sound asleep. I didn't get to bed until nearly two o'clock this morning."

"One of your children sick, or did you get hooked into watching a late T.V. movie?"

"Neither," Jim replied. "I was studying, or at least trying to study. I might as well have gone to bed at ten o'clock."

Walt thought a little humor might help, so he tried, "I didn't think you studied your Sunday School lesson 'til Saturday night, and last night was only Monday."

"It was that course I started last night at the extension center over at Calvary Church. I got home about nine and

74

thought I could knock out the assignment for Thursday night in about an hour, so I didn't start until after the ten o'clock news. I must have forgotten all I ever knew about how to study."

Now Walt tried reassurance, "I know what you mean, but it will all come back after a few weeks. The first quarter I was back at State after the Korean War, I spent more time just staring at a book than I did studying."

"I hope it will; I'll be sunk if it doesn't. I surely wish I had someone to give me a few pointers."

Anyone who has started a new learning adventure after being away from such experiences for several years is likely to feel very much as Jim did. A few pointers may help the reader to get more out of his study time.

Developing Reading Skills

The most important study skill is reading. Inability to read at all is a serious obstacle in learning. Poor reading habits hinder millions of adults who are not functional illiterates.

Skim, read, examine.—The serious reader should plan to read a book, or a selection, three times. Houle [1] traces the suggestion back three centuries to the French philosopher René Descartes. The purpose of the first reading is to learn generally the topics with which the author deals; the second, to see the development of his reasoning; and the third, to further examine questions raised by the first two readings.

One might agree that this would be a good method if he were convinced that it would take no longer than would one careful reading. A study by McClusky [2] showed that a preliminary skimming of material, followed by a serious reading, took no more reading time for comprehension than did only one reading if the reader had a general background knowledge of the field. With unfamiliar materials the results might be different. Houle [3] suggests two reasons why the "skim-read-examine" method is better for most people. First, by getting a view of the whole, it then is easier to understand each part and to see the relationship of the parts to one another and to the whole. By understanding the basic idea of the material, the reader has a better idea of what he must master and can identify beforehand those parts which will need special attention.

Second, by alternating between kinds of reading processes, the task is less likely to become monotonous. Many books lend themselves to the "skim-read-examine" method, chapter by chapter, when each chapter deals with a separate topic. In the "skimming" phase, look first at the table of contents to see what topics are included in the book. If the author has not done so, divide the book by grouping the chapters into logical units of several chapters. Read the Preface or Introduction carefully, for here the writer often shares the general plan of the book and his special points of view with the reader.

As you skim the chapters in a given unit, pay special attention to their subheadings. Some writers follow a style in which the main idea of each paragraph is stated succinctly at the beginning. Give special attention to these introductory sentences.

During the serious reading of a section, carry on a "conversation" with the author. Read as carefully as you would listen to an expert discussing the topic. Add your ideas and experience to what the writer says and form a synthesis of this information. It is helpful to try guessing what will come next or how the main thought will be developed. Ask questions of the author, then search for answers.

As you read, make a separate, written outline, underline key sentences in a section, or use a pastel felt pen and lightly mark over phrases or sentences containing main ideas. While the separate outline takes longer, having all the material on one or a few pages is an advantage. At a glance you can see the entire framework of the book. Also the outline will be valuable in deciding which sections need reviewing.

Try to discover general principles which can be inferred from the material. They will serve as a "stockpile" around which to organize separate facts or ideas. General principles can be applied in many different situations whereas a specific fact, idea, technique, or method has only limited applicability. Separate facts or procedures may have to be memorized. But if one understands the underlying principle, he can "figure out" a temporarily forgotten part in a particular application.

Do not skip over tables, charts, graphs, or pictures. "One picture is worth a thousand words." A concept or set of facts which is presented graphically or pictorially is often much easier to understand. The author will frequently depend on these to communicate information to his reader and will not make a further detailed explanation.

The third reading is for deeper study of unusually important or difficult sections. Paragraphs or sections containing the essential ideas should be reviewed. Reexamine sections where questions were raised but not answered. If you tried to forecast what was coming next as you read, restudy those sections containing surprises. They indicate that your train of thought was different from that of the author and that you may have misunderstood the point he was trying to develop.

Reading speed.—Reading speed should vary according to the type of material being read. Light fiction, that is being read mainly for relaxation, can usually be done rapidly. Except for the so-called psychological or philosophical novel, close attention to details is seldom necessary in order to understand the plot development of a story.

Materials dealing with matters such as biblical interpretation or Christian doctrines must be read more slowly for understanding. Highly specialized or technical material requires even more time per page.

A common misunderstanding is that the slow reader understands more of what he reads than does the fast reader.
Usually, for a given kind of material, the opposite is true. The
fast reader ordinarily understands and remembers more than
the slow reader. This indicates that one should read any
material as rapidly as possible and still get the sense of it.

In order to maintain reading speed, one should read a
variety of material. This is especially true if one's vocation or
profession requires reading such as legal opinions, technical
reports, contracts, or specifications. One attorney reads mur-
der mysteries as a pastime. Reading fictional cases fast in
order to see "who done it" counteracts the slowing down effect
that attention to details in real cases has on his reading speed.

A Study Schedule

When a serious study program is undertaken, a definite time
schedule for study must be set up. One who plans to study in
his spare time usually finds spare time suddenly evaporating.
Like anything worthwhile, learning costs; one cost is an in-
vestment of time. If a learning program is centered around an
organization or group with regular meeting times, that schedule will serve as a guide to a personal study schedule. If the
study is serious and the participant expects to make his pro-
portionate contribution to the group's learning experiences, a
good rule is to spend two hours in preparation for each hour
in class or with group. In some cases this much time may not
be required; in others, there may not be that much time
available for out-of-class preparation. In setting up a schedule,
be realistic.

Most adults must give their vocation and family priority
time. Learning has to be scheduled during leisure hours. It
would be unrealistic for most adults to plan to spend *all* of
their leisure time in study.

The evening hours usually are more suitable for study; but

this will depend upon the composition of the family. If there are preschool children in the family, fewer distractions occur after they have gone to bed. If the children are in school, the mother may find that her best time to study is during school hours when she is alone at home. Each person must examine his own activities schedule and determine the best time for study. If the schedule doesn't work out as planned, change it until a workable one is found. Be sure to leave some flexibility. A plan to study from seven-thirty until nine-thirty on Tuesday evening may have to be altered some Tuesday when something unforeseen occurs. Then an alternate study period should be set up at the same time the decision not to study is made. Perhaps from five-thirty to six-thirty on Thursday or ten to eleven on Friday would be good alternate hours.

The length of study periods must vary. Because of temperament or motivation, some persons are able to study for longer stretches at a time than others. Some kinds of material are easier to study longer. Recognizing these variations, there are some general rules to guide the average person in study that consists primarily of reading.

Most persons take a few minutes to prepare for study. At least forty-five minutes to an hour are needed at one time to study. In study periods longer than one and one-half or two hours, learning usually decreases per unit of time. Persons tire of an activity that is continued too long. Generally, study periods somewhere between one and two hours in length yield the greatest return in learning per hour.

If the material requires much memorizing, shorter periods of study are recommended. Voek [4] reports one study in which three groups each spent a total of two hours memorizing material. One group used the two hours in one block of time. The second group studied forty minutes at a time for three days and learned about fifty percent as much as the first group. The third group studied twelve ten minute periods for three days.

The third group learned almost twice as much as the first in the same amount of study time.

Like other factors in the study schedule, this one must be tailored to fit the individual and his study program. One good sign that the period has lasted long enough is when one's attention persistently wanders from the subject.

Few adults can study on the job. Most employers feel they are buying all of the employee's time while he is at work. However, most adults spend some time just waiting. If one rides public transportation to and from work, he probably spends an hour a day just looking out the window at the same houses, trees, buildings, and so forth. These five hours each week could be spent reading in connection with a study program. Shorter periods of time are spent waiting in barber shops, beauty shops, doctors' offices, and so on. Using these snatches of time in learning activities rather than in idleness could make the difference between a growing and a stagnant personality. These periods are best used for the "skimming" of material. They could be used for the second or third reading if one is able to underline and write in marginal notes as he reads. Few brief, "on-the-go" periods would permit note-taking, outlining, or solving mathmatical problems. Most people would be surprised if they kept for a week a record of the time spent doing nothing more than casually flipping through a magazine while waiting for someone else.

A Place to Study

A definite place to study is almost as important as a specific schedule of study. When reactivating old learning skills or developing new ones, it is especially helpful if studying can be done at the same place, and if the same room, desk or table, and chair are used *only* for study. Then, when one sits down to study, it is like saying to himself, "Okay, this is where we study; let's get on with it." If study materials can be kept

together in one place, much less "warm-up" time will be
required. After a study routine at one place has been established, it will be easier to study somewhere else if circumstances make that necessary. Just as it is best to stay close to a
time schedule, so is it best to study in one place.

A place free from distractions is certainly to be desired. A
highly motivated person is not easily distracted. One who
studies half-heartedly may be distracted even in a quiet room
by himself. A room where a television is playing, or where
other persons are engaged in non-study activities, is *not* an
ideal place to study. A radio or record player with quiet,
instrumental music may aid study, but other kinds of music or
programs decrease the study efficiency of most people, especially adults. The ideal place to study is a special room or
home library, but few homes contain such a room.

For a modest amount, most persons can purchase a used desk
and build a study center around it. Place it in a room which
can be closed off and which is as far as possible from the
center of household activities. The room should not have to be
kept in perfect order. In most homes the parents' bedroom will
probably be the best study place. The study center need not
be elaborate. A desk in the corner of one room is all the space
needed. The next most important factor is the cooperation of
the rest of the family in respecting the adult learner's time and
place of study. Interruptions on the part of a thoughtless
spouse or children can wreck the best study plans.

Study in a college or public library on a regular schedule is
desirable even though it may be necessary to keep books and
other materials in a brief case.

Seven Keys

There is no easy road to learning. It is hard work. Cyril
O. Houle [5] suggests seven helpful principles of effective learning.

Act as though you are certain to learn.—It is significant that
he uses the word "act" rather than "think" or "feel" or "believe." The famous Methodist missionary E. Stanley Jones
said, "It is easier to *act* yourself into a new way of *thinking,*
than it is to think yourself into a new way of acting." If one
begins the new learning adventure as though the outcome was
certain to be successful, it probably will be! Fear and lack of
self-confidence have taken many adult learners down to an
early defeat.

It would be foolish to assume that *all* adults can learn *all*
things equally well. Some adults could not have learned to
play the violin at sixteen, and they need not expect to at sixty.
One who failed an art course because of lack of ability in
college is not likely to become a Grandma Moses at eighty.
Numbers of studies have shown, however, that there are
many, many useful things practically any adult *can* learn. If
one really believes he cannot learn, this in itself may make
that true. One may have misgivings about a particular learning task; but, if he will begin acting as if he believes himself
able to learn, he will, by this positive attitude, soon find that
he is learning! Houle quotes a mother's advice to her daugh-
ter, about to go to her first ball and full of dread and fear, "My
dear, bite your lips to make them nice and red, throw your
shoulders back, hold your head high—and sail right in!" The
beginning learner may not need red lips, but the rest is good
advice.

Set realistic goals.—Goals should be realistic and clear. It is
important for the adult learner to be able to measure progress
toward his goal, so they need to be stated in measurable
terms, such as the number of courses or books to be completed
in one year.

Long-range goals are achieved by a series of short-term
objectives. For example, an adult enrols in a correspondence
Bible study course of sixteen lessons. He sets as his goal the

completion of the course within two months. At the end of the first week, he has finished only the first lesson. Realizing the unreality of his first goal, he revises his schedule to complete one lesson each week. Maintaining this plan, he has a feeling of achievement each Saturday as he mails another finished lesson.

With so many learning opportunities available, no adult should undertake a program of study without knowing clearly what he wants from it. If a realistic goal is clearly established and a particular course of study is designed to achieve it, the adult can expect to reach the goal.

Remember the effect of your own opinion.—One factor which the learner brings to the learning situation is his own point of view. This can be either an aid to learning or a hindrance. One study has shown that a person more accurately estimates the size of a neutral object, having little or no value to him, than he does a treasured object. He tends to overestimate the size of the latter. The greater he values the object, the larger is his error. The same tendency appears in the realm of ideas. One inclines to overestimate the importance or truth of an idea which he esteems and to undervalue the belief or opinion of a person with whom he disagrees. Both persons bring biased viewpoints to a discussion; neither can avoid it altogether. When diverse opinions are shared in a discussion, effective learning takes place if persons have open minds as well as convictions. It may be rewarding to try analyzing why they hold certain opinions. This effort often brings them nearer the truth. The adult who cannot tolerate new ideas, or people who disagree with him, is not likely to learn very much.

Relate new learning to old.—An adult's greatest learning asset is his rich background of experience. He does not have to learn everything "from scratch," but can transfer similar aspects of previous learning to the new situation. Facing a new learning task, one should ask himself, "How is this like something I've learned before? How is this essentially different from some previous learning to which it bears some similarity?" As he answers these questions, he will have "factored out" the new learning required, and its relationship to what is already known will be easier to see. This is true in learning a new skill or a new concept.

It is better to concentrate on learning general principles than specific facts only, since principles can be related to different problems or to new learning tasks.

Seek needed help.—The word "needed" should be underscored. An adult may learn more by working through the "hard places" himself rather than frequently seeking help. There are times, however, when he should seek help and support.

First, one should seek an experienced teacher when starting study in a new area. He can point out the basic skills needed, supply essential information, and demonstrate techniques. He can help one to avoid pitfalls and unnecessary detours.

Second, seek help when study "bogs down." A more experienced person can aid in discovering why one's progress suddenly slows down. Often it helps just to have another person look at the problem from another viewpoint. It is much better to seek help than to quit.

Some studying is better done alone. But when effective learning requires sharing ideas, the stimulation of a study group is needed. At such times the learner must seek help.

Overlearn.—This may sound foolish to an adult who already has a busy schedule. But if he wishes to learn something permanently, it is not enough to learn just to the point of being able to repeat it, or to do the task without error. Study and practice beyond this point are necessary. Some amateur and professional athletes are outstanding because they greatly overlearned needed skills.

Use psychological practices.—These are regarded by some

as "gimmicks." But if they work, they are useful learning tools.

When a new skill or concept is difficult to learn, go on to some other problem or activity. One unconsciously continues to work on the problem. Later the needed insight may come suddenly, and the original problem can be solved quickly.

Doing the easier tasks first gives one greater confidence as he tackles the more difficult ones later.

Jot down ideas as they pop into the mind and file them away. Some preachers build files of sermon material in this way. Do not file "good ideas" only. Sometimes, a seemingly silly idea at first, when combined with another one, may become quite sound.

Organize material in a way that is easy to remember. These memory "crutches" may help in remembering major points in an outline.

Reviewing

Some time near the end of a study period should be reserved for review. If the study period is more than one hour long, breaking the period at about the middle for a review of the study is desirable. At least five minutes of each hour's study time should be spent in reviewing. If the review is for a formal examination, memorize an outline of the material covered. At other times, this may be helpful but not necessary or worth the time and effort required. Many books and study guides have a list of questions at the end of the chapter or lesson. These questions cover material that the author (an expert in the field) considers to be most important. Look over such questions before reading a chapter, keep them in mind as the chapter is studied, then try to answer them from memory at the end of the study period.

If a chapter, lesson, or other unit is not completed at the end of a study period, review the previously studied portion at the beginning of the next study period.

Any of the author's questions that cannot be answered will indicate areas where further study and review are needed. After these have been reviewed, relate them to the whole section to get an overall view of the area. When the author has not provided review questions, search for the most important points or ideas discussed in the chapter. Make brief notes on them, then review the chapter to discover any important points that may have been overlooked or forgotten.

Frequent reviews are important and valuable when studying material that must be remembered. They also help one to discern the significant.

NOTES

1. Cyril O. Houle, *Continuing Your Education* (New York: McGraw-Hill Book Co., 1964), pp. 1–2.

2. Howard Y. McClusky, "An Experiment on the Influence of Preliminary Skimming on Reading," *Journal of Educational Psychology*, XXV (1934), pp. 421–529.

3. Houle, *op. cit.*, pp. 2–4.

4. Virginia Voeks, *On Becoming an Educated Person* (2d ed., Philadelphia: W. B. Saunders Co., 1964), p. 37.

5. Houle, *op. cit.*, pp. 17–36.

6 THE FELLOWSHIP OF LEARNING

The superintendent said something about not having the usual departmental assembly during the following month. At this Jim listened more attentively. The superintendent continued, "We will, however, meet here from nine-thirty to ten o'clock. Following a hymn and prayer, my associate, Mr. Burton, will teach the lesson to the entire department. This will be an expository lecture on the content of the Bible passages. Then you will go to your classes. Under the guidance of your teachers, you will discuss the meaning of these truths for our lives here in Centreville.

"Our teachers have agreed to try this new approach for four weeks. They will say more about it in your classes. We would like to start our experiment next Sunday. Any suggestions as to how this might be made more effective will be welcome.

"After the four weeks trial, you will decide about continuing this procedure."

Jim's first reaction was that too many changes were being introduced too quickly. Walt had taught the class for only two months, and the members were just getting used to his method. He had replaced the lectern with a small table and had hung a set of Bible land maps on the wall. Instead of lecturing, he sat down most of the time and led a discussion of the lesson. Now the fellows were studying more, accepting some advance assignments, and entering into the discussions. Jim hadn't liked that change and told Walt so on the way to work the next morning. Now, however, he admitted he was getting more out of Sunday School than ever before.

The class had started using new material. Unfamiliar with the design and format, Jim, at first, didn't like that either. But, as with Walt's teaching, he was now feeling at home with the new resource materials.

In class, when Walt more fully explained the new approach, it didn't sound so different. Walt said that each Sunday he would give the members a study guide and some questions to keep in mind as they studied for the next lesson. He explained that after the departmental teacher had covered the content of the lesson, the class would have the needed time to discuss its application.

Chuck Wood objected, "I'm just not sure that now is the best time to try this, I'm not even sure the method will work on the next lessons, Walt. I've studied a unit on the Major Prophets every five or six years since I was in the Junior Department. It never had much to say about Centreville in the twentieth century!"

"That's one reason we teachers wanted to try this new procedure," Walt replied. "We believe that the Scriptures do have something to say to our day. We will have more opportunity to discover these truths and discuss their application.

The class voted to try the new plan and suggested that the classes meet together for the last five minutes to share especially helpful truths they had discovered.

At the end of the four weeks each class met on Wednesday evening to evaluate the new approach. Afterwards, the teachers and class and departmental officers met to decide whether to continue, modify, or abandon the plan. Some classes were having good discussions following the department lesson. The decision was made to try the plan for three more months. Jim's reaction was typical. He liked some things about the lecture-discussion approach, but felt more at home with Walt doing all the teaching. But he admitted that he was studying more than he had in a long time.

Many people feel that experiments like the one just described have no place in religious education, certainly not in Sunday School. Others feel that a group learning, or group-dynamics, approach will solve all the problems of adult Christian education. There really is nothing basically new about current group learning, although recent refinement in techniques make it easier to apply long-standing principles.

The Master Teacher

Jesus was no ordinary teacher, but he taught ordinary men. He was certainly more than an effective discussion leader; he was one who could speak with absolute authority. Even so, he involved his hearers in discussions that made learning more effective. Two examples will illustrate the point.

Mark records a discussion between Jesus and his disciples (8:27-30). "Whom do men say that I am?" Jesus asked. Several of the disciples joined in the discussion. Jesus then asked them a more personal question concerning their own faith. On the basis of Peter's answer for the group, he began to teach them about his coming death and resurrection.

Luke records another discussion between Jesus and two disciples on the road to Emmaus (24:13-16). He even pretended not to know of the crucifixion in Jerusalem in order to induce them to put into words their own interpretation of the events. After this discussion, which probably lasted for several miles, Jesus began "with Moses and all the prophets" to teach them how he had fulfilled all scriptures concerning the Messiah.

In the jargon of modern education, Jesus engaged his learners in dialogue rather than simply telling them the truth. He often involved only one other person.

An early description of the church says, "They devoted

themselves to the apostles' teaching and fellowship, to the breaking of bread and the prayers" (Acts 2:42). Small groups of Christians met from house to house to plumb the depths of their new found faith in Christ.

In modern times the Wesleyan Revival started when four Oxford students met regularly to study the Scriptures, pray, "and engage in spiritual conversations." The heart of the Methodist movement was the "class meeting." "Ten members and their leaders" met "regularly for mutual encouragement, rebuke," Bible study, and prayer.[1]

Why Group Learning?

Most of a person's learning takes place in a group. For children and youth these groups include the family, the school class, neighborhood gangs, and various church and community groups. Adults, too, learn best in groups. The evidence is that they learn best by active participation in the teaching-learning process.

Learning is more probable.—"Telling is not teaching and listening is not learning." Simple recall of the content of a lecture after four or six weeks has been disappointing indeed. To grow in Bible knowledge, a person must be involved in experiences that clarify its meaning. Then the Bible becomes more helpful, providing resources for daily living and direction for life. Informal groups in which members share their experiences make this kind of learning more probable.

Reuel Howe [2] says that "the dialogical principle (i.e., the two-way conversation between teacher and learner) is the underlying assumption in education that would be Christian." Teachers who "teach by telling" soon discover that they are not being heard nor understood. Barriers to communication and learning are raised if the teacher is unaware of, or unresponsive to, the learners' thoughts and needs and when the learner is unprepared to understand and respond to the teacher's thought and words. Interaction between teacher and learner can clarify concepts and their application. Christian education must release the "full powers of both teacher and learner" in order for both to become strong and more resourceful rather than remain weak and more dependent.

Learning in fellowship.—Interaction with others is the primary influence that stimulates adults to learn. Some feeling of fellowship exists in any adult learning group. In a Christian group, each learner should be characterized by a deep concern for the growth and welfare of every other member. A significant difference in the Christian group is the presence of the Holy Spirit. He can guide both the individual and the group into all truth if his leadership is sought and followed.

Theological basis.—The doctrine of soul-competency teaches that the individual Christian under the leadership of the Holy Spirit is competent to read and interpret the Holy Scriptures for himself. The individual enters into a learning partnership with the Spirit. As he seeks diligently after the truth and uses every resource at his disposal, the Holy Spirit guides his search, discovery, and application. Each person is active in this kind of learning. Every learner, not just the teacher, should be involved in disciplined study. This belief is violated if a group of adults is assembled for Christian education and expects only the leader to carry the burden of teaching. Each person has some responsibility for the learning achievements of a study period. If one has studied and gained fresh insights he should have an opportunity to share them with the other members.

The Nature of the Adult Learner

The nature of the adult learner demands an informal approach to his religious education.

While adult groups have many needs in common, individual

needs vary. By participation in the teaching-learning process, each person has an opportunity to reveal his own needs. As these needs are shared, adults can become more sensitive and helpful to one another. The teacher or leader gains more accurate knowledge of the group and can plan better class or group sessions.

Every learning group should make the best use of its available resources. Often their own experiences are the most valuable resources a group of adult learners has. Past experiences can be related to new learning tasks as they are shared with the group. This interaction aids in clarifying new concepts or learning skills. The group limits itself unnecessarily when only the teacher shares his experiences.

The adult who thinks for himself is not likely to accept all a teacher says. His viewpoints, ideas and opinions change as he has opportunity to share them in discussions with others.

Some people seek knowledge simply out of a desire to know, apart from any value it may have for them. The ordinary adult has learned enough about the world in which he lives to satisfy mere curiosity. He now is interested in learning for its practical value. How can I use this? Will it help me be a better worker? Will it make my job easier. Can I get a better job? Will it help me to be a better Christian? parent? church member? The adult is interested in learning anything that will help him with daily needs and problems. For example, few adults seem interested in Bible study just to know more about the Bible, but they are eager to know how its message applies to their lives today.

The Christian Community

A learning group of adult Christians should be a miniature Christian community.

Concern.—A deep concern for each other was one distinctive characteristic of the early Christian community.

The sharing of joy, sorrow, faith, doubt, pleasure, pain, problems and their solutions takes place best in small groups. There, Christians are strengthened for life in a world unfriendly to Christ. In an atmosphere of redemptive concern the struggle with conflict and doubt can make one stronger in his Christian faith.

The New Testament world was impressed by the concern which Christians had for one another. People in our day are influenced when Christian concern is expressed in actions as well as words.

Trust.—Christians should share a mutual trust in one another. This characteristic is essential in the fellowship of learning. If religious education is to be dynamically related to life, each person must feel that he can trust others in the group when deep issues are involved. Trust does not come easily nor quickly; but as members of a group share testimony of the Lord's work in their lives, problems they face, and ask the prayers of the group, gradually the realization grows that one is safe in sharing anything with these Christian friends. In such an atmosphere, the most meaningful learning can take place.

Determining Directions

The importance of clearly defined goals in any learning adventure has been emphasized previously. When a shift is made from teacher-centered learning to a group learning team, the ability to formulate group goals must be developed.

Presumably, the purpose of a learning activity is some desired change in the lives of group members as a result of the study experiences. To accomplish this, certain elements must be considered: (1) the topic and resource materials to be used and (2) the needs and interests of the learners. For example, if a group decides to study a particular Christian doctrine, the teacher, scripture passages, books, and other resource material must be selected, all with some understanding of the theological interests and needs of the study group.

If there are several alternatives from which to choose topics and resource material, a vote will indicate need and interest. This can be done by providing a check list of topics and materials available and asking each one to indicate his preference.

After the group has selected the topic and materials for study, a specific goal acceptable to all group members should be formulated. This is especially important if the study is to continue for several weeks.

Several methods of determining this goal are possible. The larger group might divide into "buzz groups" (see page 96–7) and suggest goals which could then be written on a chalkboard. After discussion by the larger group, the final goal could be formulated.

Another procedure would be to ask each member to write a brief statement of what he personally would like to gain from the study. After considering these statements, a committee could then suggest a learning goal. This could be changed until it was accepted by the group.

Any procedure used should involve all members of the group. Enough time should be taken for revising to make the goal acceptable to each one.

Cartwright and Zander [3] see a clearly defined group goal as a most important motivating force for group action. They define a group goal as "an action inducing agent." Once a group goal has been agreed upon, "good" group members will work for its achievement even though it is not their preferred goal.

Many Methods

A widespread misconception about group learning approach is that it is an educational method. It is vaguely referred to as the "group discussion method." There are many group learning methods. Each is effective under certain circumstances. No one method suits all purposes; therefore, any learning group may use a variety.

One method used effectively by Dr. Gaines S. Dobbins was to ask a question, then let the class work with it until someone came up with the *right* answer. One such question was, "What is the poorest method of teaching?" As various methods were suggested, Dr. Dobbins indicated conditions under which each method could be used effectively. The *right* answer was that the poorest method of teaching is the one a teacher uses all the time. A variety of methods is needed.

Following are some methods which stimulate group interest in a topic, focus attention on significant questions, and increase participation in the discussion period.

Role-playing.—This is a variation of a very old teaching method—the drama. The "encyclical dramas and morality plays of the middle ages" basically used this technique.[4]

Role-playing is the spontaneous acting out of a situation without the benefit (or burden) of a prepared script. The situation should be plausible, true to life, and related to the topic.

The study leader first explains the purpose of role-playing, then describes in some detail the situation to be role-played. Either he or the group members select the cast, usually no more than two or three players. The leader then describes the roles to the players, giving special attention to the attitudes they are to express. There is no script or rehearsal, and very little preplanning.

Usually the actual role-playing scene is no more than five minutes. The leader interrupts the scene which then is used as a basis for discussion of the problem portrayed in the action.

No one should be forced to take part in the role-playing. However, after a group becomes familiar with the method, even the most timid person usually is willing to participate.

Role-playing could be used to train canvassers in a church budget campaign. One man plays the role of canvasser; another, the church member who seldom attends and has made no pledge to the church budget. The scene is in the home of the second player who gives all his reasons for not pledging. The canvasser answers in a helpful spirit, trying to lead the delinquent member to see his responsibility and opportunity. After about five minutes the leader stops the action, and the group evaluates the way in which the canvasser handled the situation. First, they point out the positive aspects of his approach, then suggest how he might have used different approaches.

Other uses might be for studies dealing with family problems, soul-winning, and many others.

One word of caution: roles are sometimes played so forcefully that the audience believes that the attitudes portrayed are the players' own. The leader should explain that the participants are simply *playing* these roles and may reflect opinions and attitudes which they themselves do not hold. Kuhn [5] has helpfully outlined the steps in this technique as follows:

1. Define the problem and set the scene
2. Decide on the characters to act out the problem
3. Choose group members for the roles
4. Prepare players for their roles
5. Act out the scene
6. Cut, and in some instances, replay the scene.
7. Bring group members into the discussion to analyze and evaluate the roles played and the solutions developed by players and audience.

Buzz groups.—The buzz group method usually involves every member in some level of discussion. This method may be used with as few as ten persons or as many as one hundred or more. The purpose is to utilize the full resources of the group in solving a problem or answering a question. It is important for the question or problem to be stated very clearly.

One value of buzz groups is that persons who seldom speak in a group of fifteen or more people will contribute ideas in a small group. Another factor is anonymity. A person, identified with a group, may raise a question or present an idea that he would not otherwise have voiced.

Buzz groups generally work this way:

1. The question or problem is clearly stated.

2. The larger group is divided into groups of five or six persons.

3. A chairman is selected for each group to keep it moving and on the assigned topic.

4. A secretary-reporter is selected to keep notes and report on findings.

5. The discussions continue approximately five minutes.

6. The buzz groups are recalled and the larger group is formed. The secretary-reporter and chairman of each group decide on one suggestion to present to the larger group.

7. One or two sentence reports from each group are written on the chalkboard and serve as topics for a discussion by the larger group. After being in a buzz group, people enter more readily into the larger group discussion.

"Brainstorming" is a variation of buzz-groups. Each group lists as many ideas or solutions as possible, no matter how wild or impossible they seem at the moment. This may be done at the close of one period. The lists of ideas are collected and cataloged before the next meeting. There the most promising solutions are presented for discussion, evaluation, and action.

In a symposium, the moderator briefly outlines the subject to be discussed, then presents two to four participants who make three- or four-minute speeches on the topic. The moderator and speakers should be seated informally and facing the audience. Each speaker should discuss a different aspect of the topic. It is good if *opposing* views can be presented by the speakers.

The presentations should be followed by questions, comments, and discussion by the larger group.

Panel discussion.—A panel discussion is often confused with a symposium. The major difference is that there are no speeches or introductory statements by the panel members. The moderator introduces the subject, then asks a panel member a leading question related to it. From that point on the members discuss the topic among themselves. The moderator guides the conversation by questions or comments from time to time.

After approximately one-third of the session time has elapsed, the moderator brings the larger group into the conversation with well formulated questions. The panel members and the larger group may talk back and forth, or the discussion may be between two panel members or between two members of the larger group.

The moderator should take enough time at the close of the period to summarize the discussion.

Modified debate.—The usual debate is a presentation of the affirmative and negative sides of a question, followed by a rebuttal when each debater has an opportunity to answer his opponent.

The modified debate does not use the rebuttal period. Instead, after the affirmative and negative sides have been presented, the larger group discusses the question. The moderator presides and guides the general discussion.

Topics for debate might include: Resolved: Christians should never participate in social drinking; Resolved: Baptists should maintain and strengthen their colleges; Resolved: Revival meetings are the most effective way of reaching the lost.

Summary

Jesus involved individuals and groups in two-way discussions in which views were exchanged and new insights were revealed. The early church spent much time discoursing on the apostles' teaching trying to understand the implications of their new found faith. Many religious revival movements have begun as some form of group discussions.

The renewed emphasis on group learning is based on its validity as an educational principle. As they search after truth, adults learn more readily in a fellowship of learning. Group learning has a theological basis in the doctrines of the Holy Spirit and soul-competency.

The nature and needs of an adult predispose him to learn more effectively in a group. The Christian community creates an atmosphere favorable to group learning when it is characterized by concern and trust.

The first step in group learning is to determine clearly the goals. Many methods are available to stimulate interest, focus attention, and increase participation in activities designed to accomplish the stated aims. Learning along with a group of persons of similar interests and concerns has many advantages over learning alone.

NOTES

1. John L. Casteel, *Spiritual Renewal Through Personal Groups* (New York: Association Press, 1957), pp. 12–21.

2. Reuel L. Howe, *Dialogic Foundations of Christian Adult Education* (Pittsburgh: The University of Pittsburgh Press, 1962), pp. 153–168.

3. Dorwin Cartwright and Alvin Zander, *Group Dynamics* (Evanston: Row, Peterson & Co., 1953), p. 311.

4. Margaret E. Kuhn, *You Can't Be Human Alone* (New York: The National Council of Churches, 1956), p. 21.

5. *Ibid.,* p. 22.

Walt could tell by the way Jim kept reading his paper as he came toward the car that something in it had really excited him. As Walt pulled away from the curb, Jim slapped the paper and said, "Look at that, 'Aldermen Delay Enforcement of Sunday Closing Law.' That new board is afraid to take action on anything!"

He summarized the report of the meeting. "First, the city attorney assured them that the law was constitutional, based on court decisions in two trial cases six years ago. Next, the Safety Director testified that the law was enforceable—that he now had enough patrolmen on duty to check on and issue citations to all offenders. Finally, representatives from both the Better Business Bureau and the Retail Merchants Association said that their organizations were solidly behind strict enforcement of the law. Do you know what they did after all that?"

"From the headline you read I take it they decided to delay action on it."

"Well, that is what it amounted to. They appointed a sub-committee to gather additional information and bring back a recommendation to the board at its regular meeting next month. They can hold more meetings, hear more testimony, appoint more committees, and take less action than any group I know of!"

Walt tried to get Jim to look at the other side of the local political situation, "Everything is going well in city politics right now. I guess when a real issue comes up, they have to stretch it out as long as they can. Employment is at an all-time high; crime is at an all-time low; business is good; and almost everybody is happy. They wouldn't feel like they had earned their pay if they just met, heard a report that all is well, and dismissed. They'll take action next month I'm sure."

Walt decided to change the subject. "I had a real good meeting at church last night with the group responsible for the planning of our next unit of study on the Christian's responsibility as a religious educator in the home. Some real good resource materials are available, like a set of records to stimulate discussion. We've invited Dr. Hurstbourne, the child psychologist from the University Center, to be a resource person. Our minister of education is to tell us what the children's departments are trying to do and how we can help at home."

For a moment Jim seemed excited about Walt's report, "Say, I like that. Just last week, after I had finished helping Jimmy with his Sunday School lesson, we were talking about how little we really know about what our children are studying at church. This ought to be good."

After reflecting for a moment, he added, "That is if we don't do like we do a lot of the time. You know, we are about as bad as that Board of Aldermen. We get an interesting topic, enjoy a good discussion on it, even learn a good bit about it, but we usually do nothing—absolutely nothing!"

This time Walt had an answer, "I'm glad you brought that up. That is just where we were when we had to quit last night. We hope to build some action patterns into this next unit and are meeting again Sunday afternoon to discuss ideas. Then we will probably ask the group for suggestions Sunday evening. See what you can come up with between now and then."

Jim's question is related to a central problem in adult education. How are good discussions translated into programs of action which will accomplish significant change?

In Jesus' life and ministry is seen a balance between study and action. "And he went about all Galilee, teaching in their synagogues and preaching the gospel of the kingdom and healing every disease and every infirmity among the people" (Matt. 4:23). Jesus told seventy disciples to "heal the sick in it [the town] and say to them, 'The kingdom of God has come near to you'" (Luke 10:9). After preaching and teaching about the nature of the kingdom, Jesus took action to correct a wrong use of the temple: "And he entered the temple and began to drive out those who sold, saying to them, 'It is written, "My house shall be a house of prayer"; but you have made it a den of robbers'" (Luke 19:45–46).

Jesus' action of raising Lazarus from the dead soon brought to a crisis the conflict that had long smoldered between him and the religious leaders of the Jews. Jesus spent much time in teaching, but he was also a man of deliberate action whenever that was necessary for the fulfilment of his eternal purpose.

Accent on Action

Deliberate action based on thoughtful discussion is an essential part of the learning process; it is one means of providing continuity between discussion periods. If a group discusses and arrives at a solution to a problem but does not act, both the problem and the solution are likely to be forgotten. If the plan is put into action, this experience will reinforce the discussion and will guide the group at its next meeting in planning further action. Such experiences improve the group's decision-making skills. If the action brings about desired change, some realistic basis for greater self-confidence is established.

Without follow-up action, group discussions become theoretical and unrelated to real life situations. Discussions are practical when they become the basis for action programs.

Follow-up action is necessary if study and discussion are to be effective learning activities, and it is needed in most churches and communities.

"Social action on behalf of reasoned social change is the functional *raison d'etre* (reason for being) of a modern adult education movement." [1] Effective Christian living cannot be learned by precept alone. An effective church cannot be developed merely by a statement of beliefs or principles. Changes in attitudes, insights, understandings, and patterns of behavior come mainly through experience. The best adult education takes place when action grows out of the interaction of minds engaged in dynamic discussion. As the social structure of our culture changes, new patterns of witness and ministry must be discovered by the church if it is to reach today's world. These patterns must be worked out in action, reworked on the basis of results. They cannot be mere theories of discussion groups. If Christians hope to influence and reshape our nation toward realizing God's purpose in its life, they must become involved in Christian action programs.

Dr. Harry L. Miller [2] lists six conditions for learning. Two of them relate to the necessity of action in adult learning.

"Condition IV. The student must have opportunities to practice the appropriate behavior." Often the learner remains an idle observer who really needs practice if he is to adopt the desired behavior. Ideas, concepts, and beliefs must be expressed in some form of action if they are to meaningfully affect a person's life. He "must have the opportunity to do what he is supposed to learn to do."

"Condition V. The student must get reinforcement of the correct behavior." The term "reinforcement" means that as a certain pattern of action accomplishes the goal agreed upon, a group is further motivated to continued learning and action. During the course of action that follows a discussion, the learners must have "feedback." On the basis of such information, plans of action can be altered to increase the probability of achieving the desired results. The only way a group can know whether its plan of action is an effective one is by actual practice.

Apathy Analyzed

Sooner or later most people become concerned about a condition in their church or community and feel that some action should be taken to correct it. They may act alone or may stimulate a group to action, but many times nothing is done. If action is needed, why do so many persons stop with just "a good discussion"?

There are several reasons. Aware of needed action, one may agree that "somebody ought to do something about that," then add, "I would, but I'm too busy already." Often this is not just an idle excuse; it is the truth. In many families, both the husband and wife are employed outside the home. Routine housekeeping chores must be done in the evenings and on the weekends. Regular church meetings absorb all the spare time of some people. Others are involved in community and social organizations that require attending meetings and other supporting activities.

Another reason for apathy is the general nature of the times. During frontier days men moved from one crisis or emergency to another and were accustomed to taking action. In a settled culture where routines have been established to meet daily needs no one wants to "upset the applecart." This age has been characterized as one of uninvolvement. Some church groups and Christians believe that they should not become involved in political, economic, labor-management, or social problems outside the church. Can the church be what Christ intended it to be without getting involved in the "dirty" problems of the world outside the church? Refusal to be involved in political issues, labor-management controversies, or social problems may be a safe policy, but is it the Christian policy?

Others fail to take action because they mistakenly feel that they are alone in the fight against evil. The prophet Elijah retreated from life and hid in a cave. The Lord asked, "What are you doing here, Elijah?" (1 Kings 19:9). Elijah replied that he was the only one in all Israel who had been faithful to Jehovah, and because of this his enemies were seeking his life. God sent him back into the battle assuring him that there are yet seven thousand who had "not bowed to Baal" (1 Kings 19:18). Seldom is only one person concerned about any condition. If he shares his concern with others he finds others who are willing to act. Some advantages of group action include:

1. *Combined wisdom and experience can produce a more effective plan of action.*

2. *An organization with power to act will usually take more seriously a protest or suggestion from a group than from an individual.*

3. *Some risks may be involved, and these will be shared by group members.*

4. *Action based on sound Christian principles may overcome obstacles.*

If one would lead a group to overcome its natural apathy for action, he must understand some of the reasons why people resist change. They fear disorganization. While things remain the same, people know what to expect and what is expected of them. Their lives have unity and stability which provide a sense of security. Action which might bring about change creates an uncertain situation in which one does not know what to expect. The unknown may cause fear and anxiety. To avoid these unpleasant emotions, the person resists change.

Personal interests cause persons to resist change. Changes in organizational structure, in procedure, in program or curriculum may threaten one's position of leadership and result in a loss of status.

Conflicting interests may block action. People may recognize the need for action and change, but they let tradition stand in the way of progress. The usual reaction is "but we have always done it like this." Persons may resist taking action because of involvement in several groups or organizations. Benefits for one group may conflict with the interests of another. Unfortunately, units within a church may fail to take action which would benefit the whole church because that organization is not directly aided.

Not all resistance to action and change is negative in nature. It may indicate that goals are not clearly defined, or that they are not accepted by all members of a group. Resistance may also indicate a lack of communication or insufficient information. This may have a healthy effect. If opposition to action is the result of premature or inadequate planning, a reassessment is likely to result in the adoption of a more adequate final plan.

Overcoming Obstacles

After analyzing the reasons for inaction, plans should be made to overcome obstacles, and adequate planning may be the means of avoiding them altogether.

Adequate information.—A group is justified in hesitating to take action when it feels that it does not have adequate information. The leader is responsible for providing information. This may be done in several ways. The more varied the methods of presentation, the more effective it will be. Information may be presented verbally by an individual, a group, or a panel. It may be necessary to bring in resource persons who are specialists in the area of the needed information. Information should be presented visually if at all possible. Posters, charts, and graphs need not be professionally prepared, but they do need to present the information clearly. Slides or 8mm. movies are especially valuable if the planned action is at some distant place, and the group is unable to make an inspection. Churches which are considering the establishment of a mission in another part of the city have used slides and movies of the area to supply information to their congregations.

If the confidence of the group is to be maintained, full information must be presented. It would be unethical to present only information favoring action and to withhold information which might be the basis for a decision not to act or to delay action. An uninformed people are likely to oppose what they do not understand.

Provide for discussion.—After the basic information has been presented, ample time should be allowed for full discussion of all relevant issues. Without such provision, opposition, which in reality is to the procedure, may be directed toward the recommended action. Adults having opinions, relevant questions, and additional information should be given ample opportunity to present and discuss them. Time spent in discussion before action may save much more time later. Also, it will build group morale.

Strive for unity.—It is essential for action goals to be clearly stated. If all, or at least an overwhelming majority, of the members are not in agreement, the goals should be revised until this is accomplished. Buzz groups followed by open discussion may be an effective technique.

Conflicts between group members must be resolved before action is taken. Apparent conflict is often a lack of understanding. A panel discussion in which opposing views are presented may effect a reconciliation. If the conflict can be focused on one issue, role-playing could clarify it and produce agreement.

Plan in specific detail.—What is the group expected to do? What will be the responsibilities of sub-groups and individual members? For example: If a religious survey of the community is the project, the exact territory should be defined, the responsibility of each participant explained, the need for the survey presented, and the value of the undertaking to the participating group and to the community shown. Plans should be comprehensive, realistic, and attainable.

Appropriate Action

Following are some suggested helps for adult education groups.[3]

Educational in nature.—Any action project undertaken by a group that is basically educational should help it attain stated learning goals. The persons involved should become better informed about the nature of the problem. The action should develop needed skills. As a result of this experience the group would be expected to learn better how to plan and work together on future projects.

Approached experimentally.—No group can expect to know the right answer until it is tried out in action. The approach should therefore remain flexible. As each phase of a plan is completed and evaluated, the next part can be reviewed and probably improved. This procedure is essential to the learning experience.

Act in collaboration.—The decision to act and the plan of action should be by consent of the entire group and not just a few idividuals. The activity ought to involve as many members as possible. The most effective action is based on the enthusiastic commitment of all participants.

Summary

Adults become impatient with organizations which spend all their time in discussion and planning but never act. Action that follows discussion is essential for the most effective learn-

ing. Ideas and plans can best be evaluated after they are put
into action. Feedback after action helps a group to clarify its
thinking and improve its skill in working together.

Worthy action projects are likely to meet with some obstacles. These include indifference, heavy work schedules, un-
willingness to become involved, a feeling of aloneness in one's
concern, and insufficient information about needs and plans.

These obstacles can be overcome by careful planning and
democratic leadership if tested guidelines to action are followed.

NOTES

1. Paul H. Sheats, et al., *Adult Education* (New York: The Dryden
Press, 1953), pp. 496–499.

2. Harry L. Miller, *Teaching and Learning in Adult Education* (New
York: The Macmillan Co., 1964), pp. 37–50.

3. *Taking Community Action,* Leadership Pamphlet #3 (Chicago:
Adult Education Association, 1956).

8 RESOURCES ARE AVAILABLE

Bad weather had forced a change in picnic plans for the families of Jim and Walt. Not to be outdone by the weather, they had decided to have a planned potluck supper at Jim's house. As Walt's family arrived, the children headed straight for the playroom in the basement to find Jim's children. As the noise died down Alice heard the familiar music of the "Hallelujah Chorus" coming from the living room. She remarked, "Oh, you have some new records. We have wanted that album for sometime."

"Well, yes and no," replied Jane. "We have some new records, but we didn't buy them."

Alice exclaimed, "Don't tell me you have taken up shoplifting—and religious records at that!"

"Sure, and I walked right out under the librarian's eye with them, too. No. seriously, we checked them out of the Centreville Public Library. We have three albums and can keep them for two weeks.

"The library!" exclaimed Alice. "I didn't know they had anything but books."

"You have as many surprises in store for you as I had. Why, you can even check out a record player if you don't have one. To tell you the truth, I got caught in the rain and ran into the library to wait until the shower was over. The librarian asked if I wanted to check out an umbrella, and that was the beginning of a long tour of the library. I found out a lot of things I didn't know before."

The conversation drifted from one subject to another as Jane and Alice finished their combined supper.

As they sat at the table Walt noticed a new painting hanging on the dining room wall. "Say that's quite a picture you have there."

"Well, like the records, we checked it out of the library for a couple of weeks," Jim replied.

"Don't tell me you got this roast at the library, too," said Walt as he tasted it.

"No, there are a few things they don't have to lend down there. Anyway, I'm afraid there wouldn't be much left to return when we get through with that roast."

Facilities of public, college, and church libraries are available to the adult interested in learning. Unawareness of such resources and failure to use them probably prevents many adults from enjoying lifelong learning. Resources available both to groups and to a person studying alone will be considered.

Persons as Resources

A resource person is often thought of as the "outside expert" with special skills or information. Often, group members themselves are useful resource persons.

Within the group.—One advantage which any adult learner brings to a new learning task is his rich background of experience. This advantage is multiplied in a group. In considering its resources a group should take an inventory of the experiences and capabilities of its members. Upon returning to Nazareth, Jesus observed, "A prophet is not without honor except in his own country and in his own house" (Matt. 13:57). His words might be paraphrased, "An adult is not without value as a resource person except in his own learning group."

Outside the group.—If no member has the needed skill or

information, the group is justified in looking for an outside resource person. But it should exhaust its own resources first.

In most communities are dedicated Christians with professional training in many areas. Usually it is not necessary to choose between a qualified expert and an active churchman. An expert who is not sympathetic toward the learning goals of a Christian group is less valuable than one who is. Such persons might include attorneys, physicians, public school teachers, social workers, government and governmental agencies personnel, and local college faculty members.

The time of such persons usually is very limited. They should be brought in only when needed and released as soon as possible.

Presco Anderson [1] discourages the use of "stars," or self-styled experts who demand the spotlight. "Leaders should seek resource people who are skilled in the techniques of human relations, who have a genuine liking for people and a sympathetic understanding of the problems confronting the group members."

Resource Centers

One recently established university does not use the word "library" to designate a building on the campus. Because of the many and varied resources which it makes available to the student, the more descriptive term "Learning Resources Center" has been chosen. Since many libraries now contain a vast array of audio-visual aids to learning in addition to books, some more inclusive name is appropriate.

Each church should provide a learning resources center, or church library, for the use of its members. This is an increasing need. Curriculum for all age groups call for extra curricular resources in planning for learning experiences. In addition to books for individual and group study and for leisure time reading, such a center should make available slides, filmstrips, slide and film projectors, films, sound movie projectors, blank and prerecorded tapes, tape recorders, records and record players, and other equipment as needed. Films and prerecorded tapes could be borrowed through the church library from other resource centers.

Public libraries, college and university libraries, and specialized libraries may be used. Some church associations, local councils of churches, and other such organizations now maintain some kind of resource centers in a joint effort.

Governmental agencies, especially county and state departments of public health, have resources available to study groups.

Printed Resource Material

Libraries have extended their services beyond being book depositories, but books remain their most valuable learning resource.

Usually the resource person whom a group would most like to have "has already said it in an article or a book. So why not invite him in print?" [2] The most valuable use of books requires continuity. Preferably a group should study an entire book, but using relevant sections or chapters may be adequate in some instances.

If printed curriculum materials are provided for a study group, their resources should be exhausted before seeking extracurricular materials. Curriculum materials can guide the selection of other valuable resources and how to obtain them.

In addition to books, printed materials will include many periodicals. Church libraries may have back issues of curriculum and leadership periodicals, theological journals, and other religious publications. Public and college libraries also will have a large periodical section including current and back issues of popular magazines, religious, educational, and professional journals.

A wide variety of printed material for free distribution is also available. This includes pamphlets, booklets, and sometimes books. Many denominational agencies provide free materials related to their responsibilities. Booklets on health, mental health, developmental psychology, childrearing, and all phases of family living may be obtained from departments of health or directly from the United States Department of Health, Education, and Welfare.

One may need help in locating these printed materials. Most libraries maintain a subject index where all that the library has on a topic will be listed under that subject. If one is unfamiliar with such an index, the librarian will explain it.

If a local library does not have a book or periodical, it can usually be obtained on an interlibrary loan for a limited period of time.

If extracurricular materials need to be ordered from some distance or obtained through an interlibrary loan, a minimum of two weeks should be allowed for receiving them.

Coordinated printed materials such as flip charts, sentence strips, graphs, charts, and posters are a feature of many religious education courses.

Electronic Aids

Many books for the blind or the partially sighted person are now available on disc records or tapes. Entire books, including many of the Bible, have been recorded. These would be useful to one who was unable to read because of some visual defect.

Sets of slides, filmstrips with disc or tape recorded scripts, and sound movies can supply needed information quickly and effectively. As aids to learning, they should be used with a personal study program or group discussion. Audio-visual aids seldom are adequate for a complete learning experience. The most valuable ones are those which have been specifically produced for use with a given curriculum.

The best source of these aids for adult religious education groups is the denominational bookstore. Many state universities maintain an audio-visual aids center containing a wide variety of educational films. Within the state, these are lent freely or for a small rental fee. Most state departments of health have a film library and will furnish a catalog upon request.

An increasing number of discussion tapes and records are being made available—brief lectures, symposiums, or panel discussions. Such tapes and records define and clarify a problem or question, raise related subproblems, and supply some basic information, but do not suggest solutions. Their function is the same as that of a live lecture, symposium, or panel discussion—to stimulate interest and discussion of the problem, not to solve it. After the tape or record is played, the group continues the discussion. Many adult education programs, both religious and nonreligious, are producing aids which are correlated with a specific curriculum. Some, on topics of general interest would have limited use. Others afford good background material for discussions.

Other Resources

No attempt is made here to give an exhaustive list of resources and opportunities in continual learning, but the interested adult may wish to investigate the following:

Correspondence and extension courses.—A number of denominational colleges offer off-campus courses in extension centers. The courses tend to major in religion with some work in English and education. While most of these courses are not applicable toward a college degree, some schools do offer credit in the area of education. The registrar of a particular college could furnish information concerning its programs.

One denomination offers correspondence courses in all fifty states and several overseas countries. Courses are limited to biblical, theological, historical, and practical studies, and are open to ministers and laymen without any academic prerequisites. Limited credit is allowed toward a seminary diploma course.

A noncredit home Bible study course by correspondence is also available.

All states have at least one land-grant college with state-wide educational services. In the past these have been concerned chiefly with agricultural and home economic subjects for people in rural areas. Now the scope is being broadened to include off-campus classes, correspondence courses, special short-term institutes, and other work both for credit and non-credit.

In some states there now is a system of community colleges most of which offer some noncredit work to adults without academic prerequisites.

Community agencies.—Many community agencies—YMCA, YWCA, family service agencies, community centers, and settlement houses—offer opportunities in adult education. New programs projected by the federal government will probably increase these opportunities in coming years, and alert citizens should take advantage of them.

Educational Television.—Many states are developing an educational television network which will carry programs throughout the state. Most of them will be related to the state university's education extension program. Some college credit courses will likely be offered when this system is fully developed.

In many communities more opportunities and resources are available than people can use. The problem for most adults will be to choose which course or program of study will be most beneficial to him. For the Christian it should be one which would best equip him to share more effectively in the total ministry of his local church.

NOTES

1. Presco Anderson, "Using Resource People," *Conducting Workshops and Institutes,* Leadership Pamphlet #9 (Chicago: Adult Education Association, 1956), p. 29.

2. John Walker Powell, "When Books Participate," *How to Lead Discussions,* Leadership Pamphlet #1 (Chicago: Adult Education Association)

9 THE CHALLENGE OF CHANGE

It was Jim's week to drive to work, so the conversation started with something other than the morning paper's headlines. Jim and his family had spent the weekend in his hometown.

As Walt got in the car, Jim asked, "How were things at church yesterday?"

"Fine, but we missed your family. How was your trip?"

"Pretty good," replied Jim. "We enjoyed seeing the folks. My brother, both our sisters, and their families were there. It was really a good weekend. But you know things have really changed around there."

"How is that?" asked Walt.

"Well, as we drove into town I noticed the wooded area along the creek where I used to hunt and fish had been cleared out and filled in. A hundred-home subdivision is being built out there. The furniture factory is being doubled in size, and work on a new hosiery mill will start next month."

Walt responded, "Sounds like the place is really growing. I'm sure you enjoyed going back to your home church."

"Yeah, but even that is changing. Yesterday was the first day the congregation met in a new auditorium. The old one is being torn down already to build another educational building. It's just not the same church it was when I left to go to college. And you should see those fellows I finished high school with, they have really changed! I just could not believe my own eyes."

Walt grinned, "And how about yourself? Are you the same fellow who left there fifteen years ago?"

Jim had to admit, "No, I guess I've changed a little too."

Both men realized that several changes had been made recently at the plant where they worked. Operations on the assembly line had been automated. Quality control now was largely by a battery of electronic computers. Many accounting and engineering operations were done by other computers. All of this had happened within the last five years.

Jim readily noticed changes in his boyhood town because he had been away for some time. Many changes had taken place in Centreville also. But, being a part of the gradual process, he had seen them as signs of progress and had failed to notice them particularly.

In this changing world, what is the Christian's responsibility? Believing that "Jesus Christ is the same yesterday and today and for ever" (Heb. 13:8), is the Christian to resist all change?

Many pastors and laymen are concerned about the decreasing influence of the church. They believe that Christ and the gospel do not change, but that the church must find new ways to perform its ministry, that laymen especially must find new ways to express their faith.

David J. Ernsberger, a Presbyterian pastor and recognized authority in adult Christian education, sees the challenge of change in adult religious education tasks. He says, "The predominant and prevailing pattern of adult education in the church today is essentially irrelevant to the true mission of the church. . . . A case can be made for the contention that it is not only irrelevant but that it is also in outright conflict with the biblical understanding of the church's mission." [1] He thinks that most church programs of adult education train adults in tasks they are to perform *within* the church and its educational organizations. He believes that the main mission of the church is to witness and minister in the world *outside* the church.

He concludes that for the average layman "the world of daily work has no intrinsic connection with the work of the church." In a recorded interview a draftsman for an automobile firm in Detroit said, "Well, yes I think a lot about Christianity. After all I'm on the church board and of course we go to church on Sunday. But weekdays when I'm at work—I'm a draftsman—well, I don't see any connection. What's Christianity got to do with a drafting board? I see no Christian significance in my work at all." This man probably speaks for a large proportion of lay people in churches of all denominations.[2]

Ernsberger also sees a need for emphasizing and improving programs of adult education in the area of Christian family living. Religious beliefs, values, and moral codes are formed mostly in the home, even in our changing culture. In a survey among Christian parents, 86.2 percent wanted most for their children to remember "the loving, happy relationships within the family, relationships characterized by helpfulness, sympathy, and respect." Only 17 percent most wanted their children to remember "the Christian faith that unified the family, an awareness of God's guidance and love, or service to persons outside the family." He concludes that this survey points up a need "for discussion groups in which parents may be led to grasp some of the theological implications in their family relationships." [3]

Dr. Findley B. Edge is among those who are deeply concerned by the ineffectiveness of the church's educational ministry today, and he is strongly convinced that new patterns of ministry and witness must be found. He advocates a new philosophy of Christian education based on a New Testament theology. The major task of the ordained ministry would be to train and equip the laity to perform the ministry of the church in the world outside the church. Like Ernsberger, he sees this ministry focusing chiefly in the layman's daily occupational associations and in his home relationships. Some radical changes are needed in religious education if its goal of a regenerate church membership growing toward full Christian maturity is to be realized.[4]

David R. Hunter [5] sees religious education facing three choices of emphases: (1) preparing people for the future only or ministering to them where they are now, (2) transmitting a culture or equipping Christians to be agents of cultural change, (3) depending upon man-made programs or upon God indwelling the church in the person of the Holy Spirit. The second of these choices is relevant to our changing culture.

It is not sufficient for religious education simply to transmit from one generation to the next our rich Christian heritage. It is not enough to dwell only on the mighty acts of God in the past. Religious education must certainly do these things, but it must go further and equip men and women to "become a part of the Christian process which changes culture."

The Christian faith "does not exist primarily to perpetuate itself as a religion" nor the church to maintain its institutional structure. Its reason for being is "the task of overcoming the world in which it lives and of which it is a part."

Every Christian has a dual citizenship, in this world and in the kingdom of God. "In his behaviour at any one moment he is conforming essentially to the demands of his citizenship in the one or the other. Also in every moment of interaction he is some kind of an change agent. Either he is contributing to the further watering down of the Christian way of life (which goes far beyond morals) or he is enabling the power of God through his life to affect and change an essentially Godless culture."

If these men have analyzed accurately the challenge which the church faces in the changing culture of the mid-twentieth century, every adult Christian faces an equal challenge to "press on toward the goal for the prize of the upward call of God in Christ Jesus" (Phil. 3:14). The attaining of this goal will mean making Christian learning a lifelong task. It will involve difficult changes and conflict with an essentially Godless culture, but one will participate significantly in the ministry to which our Lord has called every Christian. The serious Christian has no choice but to follow this course.

In the closing scene of the play *Family Portrait*, Mary and Joseph are explaining to Leban, a suitor of Jesus' younger sister, what happened to their son.

JOSEPH: And then he was always the guest of the local synagogue. He'd preach there on Sabbaths.

LEBAN: He was a rabbi?

MARY: Not a regular rabbi.

SIMON: They called him that.

MARY: He wasn't interested in what people called him. That was one of the things he tried to teach his disciples. . . .

LEBAN: What did he teach?

MARY: Why—to love your enemies—never to judge or condemn anyone—to be *forgiving*. And to make life as easy as you could for other people. (*pauses, groping for the most important things.*) To live for a purpose in which you believe and never let anyone keep you from your belief—not even your own family. You must be willing to die for it. And not to be afraid of people who—kill the body. Because, after that, there is nothing more they can do. (*A pause . . .*) And to remember always that human life is beautiful—and noble—because it houses God. . . . I mean—when—when you degrade or dishonor human life—you degrade and dishonor God . . . (*Silence*) That was all he taught.

LEBAN: Has anyone ever tried it—to live the way he taught?

MARY: I don't think so.

LEBAN: Might be interesting to see what would happen if they did." [6]

This is the Christian's challenge in the midst of a changing culture.

NOTES

1. Ernsberger, *op. cit.*, p. 13.
2. *Ibid.*, p. 35.
3. *Ibid.*, p. 117.
4. Edge, *A Quest for Vitality in Religion*, pp. 71–74; 94–108.
5. David R. Hunter, "The Theology of Christian Education," *Religious Education*, LVIII, No. 1 (Jan-Feb., 1963), pp. 4–11.
6. Lenore Coffee and William J. Cowen, *Family Portrait* (Boston: Baker's Plays, 1940), pp. 125–128. (Quoted in Clemmons, *op. cit.*, pp. 104–105.

FOR FURTHER READING

Cartwright, Dorwin and Zander, Alvin. *Group Dynamics.* Evanston: Row, Peterson & Co., 1953.

Casteel, John L. *Spiritual Renewal Through Personal Groups.* New York: Association Press, 1957.

Edge, Findley B. *A Quest for Vitality in Religion.* Nashville: Broadman Press, 1963.

————. *Teaching for Results.* Nashville: Broadman Press, 1956.

Ernsberger, David J. *Education for Renewal.* Philadelphia: Westminster Press, 1965.

Grattan, C. Hartley. *In Quest of Knowledge.* New York: Association Press, 1955.

Houle, Cyril O. *Continuing Your Education.* New York: McGraw-Hill Book Co., 1964.

Kidd, J. R. *How Adults Learn.* New York: Association Press, 1959.

Little, Lawrence C. (ed.). *The Future Course of Christian Adult Education.* Pittsburgh: University of Pittsburgh Press, 1959.

Sherrill, Lewis J. *The Rise of Christian Education.* New York: The Macmillan Co., 1944.

Thorndike, Edward L. *Adult Interests.* New York: The Macmillan Co., 1935.

———. *Adult Learning.* New York: The Macmillan Co., 1936.

Trueblood, Elton. *The Company of the Committed.* New York: Harper & Bros., 1961.

Vinacke, W. Edgar, *The Psychology of Thinking.* New York: McGraw-Hill Book Co., 1952.

Voeks, Virginia. *On Becoming an Educated Person.* (2d ed.). Philadelphia: W. B. Saunders Co., 1964.